COGNITIVE PHENOMENOLOGY

Phenomenology is about subjective aspects of the mind, such as the conscious states associated with vision and touch, and the conscious states associated with emotions and moods, such as feelings of elation or sadness. These states have a distinctive first-person "feel" to them, called their phenomenal character. In this respect they are often taken to be radically different from mental states and processes associated with thought.

This is the first book to fully question this orthodoxy and explore the prospects of cognitive phenomenology, applying phenomenology to the study of thought and cognition. Does cognition have its own phenomenal character? Can introspection tell us either way? If consciousness flows in an unbroken "stream" as William James argued, how might a punctuated sequence of thoughts fit into it?

Elijah Chudnoff begins with a clarification of the nature of the debate about cognitive phenomenology and the network of concepts and theses that are involved in it. He then examines the following topics:

- introspection and knowledge of our own thoughts
- phenomenal contrast arguments
- the value of consciousness
- the temporal structure of experience
- the holistic character of experience and the interdependence of sensory and cognitive states
- the relationship between phenomenal character and mental representation.

Including chapter summaries, annotated further reading, and a glossary, this book is essential reading for anyone seeking a clear and informative introduction to and assessment of cognitive phenomenology, whether philosophy student or advanced researcher. It will also be valuable reading for those in related subjects such as philosophy of mind, philosophy of psychology and epistemology.

Elijah Chudnoff is Associate Professor of Philosophy at the University of Miami, USA. He is the author of Intuition (2013).

NEW PROBLEMS OF PHILOSOPHY
Series Editor: José Luis Bermúdez

'Routledge's *New Problems of Philosophy* series has a most impressive line-up of topical volumes aimed at upper-level undergraduate and graduate students in philosophy and at others with interests in cutting edge philosophical work. The authors are influential figures in their respective fields and notably adept at synthesizing and explaining intricate topics fairly and comprehensively.'

–John Heil, Monash University, Australia, and
Washington University, St Louis, USA

'This is an outstanding collection of volumes. The topics are well chosen and the authors are outstanding. They will be fine texts in a wide range of courses.'

–Stephen Stich, Rutgers University, USA

The New Problems of Philosophy series provides accessible and engaging surveys of the most important problems in contemporary philosophy. Each book examines a topic or theme that has emerged on the philosophical landscape in recent years, or that is a longstanding problem refreshed in light of recent work in philosophy and related disciplines. Clearly explaining the nature of the problem at hand and assessing attempts to answer it, books in the series are excellent starting-points for undergraduate and graduate students wishing to study a single topic in depth. They will also be essential reading for professional philosophers. Additional features include chapter summaries, further reading and a glossary of technical terms.

Also available:

Analyticity
Cory Juhl and Eric Loomis

Noncognitivism in Ethics
Mark Schroeder

Fiction and Fictionalism
Mark Sainsbury

Moral Epistemology
Aaron Zimmerman

Physicalism
Daniel Stoljar

Embodied Cognition
Lawrence Shapiro

COGNITIVE PHENOMENOLOGY

Elijah Chudnoff

Routledge
Taylor & Francis Group

LONDON AND NEW YORK

First published 2015
by Routledge
2 Park Square, Milton Park, Abingdon, Oxon OX14 4RN

and by Routledge
711 Third Avenue, New York, NY 10017

Routledge is an imprint of the Taylor & Francis Group, an informa business

British Library Cataloguing in Publication Data
A catalogue record for this book is available from the British Library

Library of Congress Cataloging in Publication Data
Chudnoff, Elijah.
Cognitive phenomenology / by Elijah Chudnoff.
pages cm. -- (New problems of philosophy)
Includes bibliographical references and index.
1. Phenomenology. 2. Cognition. 3. Thought and thinking. 4. Philosophy of mind. 5. Consciousness. I. Title.
B829.5.C48 2015
142'.7--dc23
2014035448

ISBN: 978-0-415-66024-2 (hbk)
ISBN: 978-0-415-66025-9 (pbk)
ISBN: 978-1-315-77192-2 (ebk)

Typeset in Joanna
by Taylor & Francis Books
Printed in Great Britain by Ashford Colour Press Ltd, Gosport, Hants

For Bohyun Kim

Behold, when we read this one precept: Love your neighbor as yourself (Mt. 22:39), three kinds of vision occur: one through the eyes, by which we see the letters themselves; another through the human spirit, by which we think of the neighbor, even when absent; and a third through an attending of the mind, by which we understand and see love itself.

St. Augustine

CONTENTS

ACKNOWLEDGEMENTS

In October of 2008 Terry Horgan and Uriah Kriegel hosted a workshop at the University of Arizona on Phenomenal Intentionality. I delivered an early version of "Intellectual Gestalts." The other speakers were: Farid Masrour, Michelle Montague, Alva Noë, David Pitt, Susanna Siegel, Charles Siewert, and Galen Strawson. There was lots of discussion about cognitive phenomenology. Much of my own thinking about the topic developed in reflection on the arguments, distinctions, examples, and views first brought to my attention on this occasion. I would like to thank all involved for stimulating my interest in cognitive phenomenology and providing rich material for further thought about it.

Between November of 2011 and November of 2013 I had the pleasure of participating in four different workshops and a seminar at Fribourg University. Some of these dealt with material that went into my earlier book on intuition. Some dealt with material that has made it into this book. All were rewarding occasions for philosophical discussion. I would like to thank Fabian Dorsch, Fiona Macpherson, Anne Meylan, Jacob Naito, Martine Nida-Rümelin, and Gianfranco Soldati for organizing and contributing to them. In the seminar Jacob Naito introduced me to the issues dealt with in chapter 4. The last workshop was dedicated to cognitive phenomenology; there I met and benefited from discussion with Tim Bayne and Peter Forrest.

Thanks to David Bourget, Terry Horgan, Uriah Kriegel, Angela Mendelovici, Michele Montague, Martine Nida-Rümelin, David Pitt, Charles Siewert, Declan Smithies, and Galen Strawson for helpful discussions about cognitive phenomenology in various other settings and over email. Thanks to Tim Bayne, Charles Siewert, and an anonymous reader for generous written comments on an earlier draft of the book that helped bring this hopefully better one about. Thanks to Azenet López for helping me prepare the manuscript for publication. And thanks to Tony Bruce and Adam Johnson for their editorial guidance.

INTRODUCTION

Imagine being in the following situations:

[Understanding] You are trying to read the instructions for a medicine a veterinarian prescribed for your dog. At first it is illegible. Then you see that it says to administer the medicine twice daily for one week.

[Intuiting] In a book you read, "If $a < 1$, then $2 - 2a > 0$," and you wonder whether this is true. Then you "see" how a's being less than 1 makes $2a$ smaller than 2 and so $2 - 2a$ greater than 0.

[Seeing] You are looking for your dogs in the dog park. At first you cannot pick them out of the mass of other dogs. But then you see them there chasing a tennis ball.

[Reacting] In the news, you read about a factory building collapsing on Bangladeshi garment workers who were ordered to work despite warnings about the safety of the building. This makes you sad and angry.

In the first two of these situations there is a change in cognitive state. At first you do not understand or intuit. And then you do. In the second two of these situations there is a change in broadly sensory state. At first you do not see or emotionally react. And then you do.

In all of these situations there is a change in phenomenal state. There is something it is like for you before understanding, intuiting, seeing, or reacting. There is something it is like at the moment of understanding, intuiting, seeing, or reacting. And what it is like before being in these mental states is different from what it is like while being in these mental states.

The main question in the recent literature on cognitive phenomenology is, to a first approximation, this: are the changes in phenomenal state exhibited in the first two cases different in kind from the changes in phenomenal state exhibited in the second two cases? Proponents of cognitive phenomenology say yes. They believe in cognitive phenomenal states. Opponents say no. According to them, all phenomenal states are sensory states.

This book is about this question and the network of philosophical issues that arise in thinking about it. In the next section I discuss some motivations for pursuing it. In the two sections after, I clarify some terminology and distinguish some of the main theses to be considered.

Motivation

Why bother about cognitive phenomenology?

One way to approach this question is to focus on the larger philosophical context. The idea is that cognitive phenomenology is worth exploring because of its significance for other areas of philosophy. There are reasons to think that the status of cognitive phenomenology bears on issues in epistemology, value theory, and semantics for example. I will say something about each of these. The topics I touch on deserve much more discussion than I can provide here. The aim is not to say anything final about any of them. Rather, it is simply to provide some philosophical context for the detailed investigation of cognitive phenomenology to be pursued in the sequel.[1]

Epistemology. Suppose you want to know whether there is mail in your mailbox. The obvious thing to do is to look. Suppose you do and see mail there. In that case you gain justification for thinking there is mail in your mailbox. Suppose instead, however, that just as you look into your mailbox something prevents the information working its way through your visual system to make any difference to how things visually appear to you. In this case you fail to gain justification for thinking there is mail in your mailbox. Even if the same visually detected information about your environment is represented somehow in your brain, if it makes no phenomenal difference, then it makes no epistemic difference.

Now consider the case of [Intuiting] (from the above list). You wonder whether if $a < 1$, then $2 - 2a > 0$. The obvious thing to do is to think about it. Suppose you do and come to "see" that if $a < 1$, then $2 - 2a > 0$. In that case you gain justification for thinking that if $a < 1$, then $2 - 2a > 0$.

There are two claims it is natural to make about this justification. First, in one way, it is different from the kind of justification you have for thinking that there is mail in your mailbox. In particular, it is a priori. That means it does not constitutively depend on sensory experiences. Even if there were sensory goings-on leading up to your acquisition of justification for believing that, if $a < 1$, then $2 - 2a > 0$, these sensory goings-on do not constitute the justification you acquired. Second, though there is this difference, there is also a way in which the justification is similar to the kind of justification you have for thinking that there is mail in your mailbox. In particular, it is phenomenal. That means it does constitutively depend on some kind of experience. Suppose that you think through the question of whether, if $a < 1$, then $2 - 2a > 0$, and all the pieces are in place, but then, just as you are about to "see" the truth, nothing new happens phenomenally. There is no phenomenal difference associated with the "seeing" over and above whatever came before. Even if all the cognitively mined information about the relevant arithmetical relations is represented somehow in your brain, if it makes no phenomenal difference, then it makes no epistemic difference.

Suppose that all phenomenal states are sensory states. Then there is a serious problem. We'd find ourselves with the following commitments: your justification for believing that if $a < 1$, then $2 - 2a > 0$ is not constituted by sensory experience, but it is constituted by some experience, and all experiences are sensory experiences. Something has to give.

Some philosophers will reject the connection between justification and phenomenology. Maybe in general, or maybe just in the case of your justification for thinking that if $a < 1$, then $2 - 2a > 0$. Other philosophers will reject the idea that any justification is independent of sensory experience – i.e. reject the a priori. This is certainly a familiar view in recent epistemology. But another option is to challenge the view that all phenomenal states are sensory states. Then there can be partly phenomenally constituted a priori justification. Figuring out to what extent this is workable requires getting clearer about cognitive phenomenology. Hence there is some motivation from epistemology to pursue such a project.

Value theory. In general stepping on a pin is bad. In some cases it might be bad because the pin is a special one that ought not be stepped on. In other cases it might be bad because the pin is a dirty one stepping on which will, unless precautions are taken, lead to further complications. In most cases, however, stepping on a pin is bad because it hurts. Take one of those cases. Now imagine a variant: you step on the pin but something prevents it from hurting. Given that the pin is neither special nor dirty and given that you didn't feel any pain, it seems that in this case stepping on the pin isn't bad, or at least not that bad. Even if the same physical and physiological events occur, if they make no phenomenal difference, then they make no difference to one's welfare, or at least not the same difference.

Now consider those aspects of your life that do not consist in keeping your feet away from pins. You think about philosophical theses, solve logical puzzles, contemplate the structures of arguments, etc. This is your intellectual life. And various events in it contribute to your welfare.

There are two claims it is natural to make about at least some of these events. First, in one way, their contribution to your welfare is different from the kind of contribution made by stepping on a pin. In particular, it is constitutively independent of sensory experience. Even if events in your intellectual life are associated with sensory goings-on, these are incidental to the values, or at least the distinctive values, they realize. We do not have a name like "a priori" for this. But the idea is similar. Second, there is also a way in which their contribution is similar to the kind made by stepping on a pin. In particular, it is phenomenal: it does constitutively depend on some kind of experience. Suppose you think through a logical puzzle, one that you take up just for enjoyment, and arrive at the solution. But nothing new happens phenomenally. The solution is stored in your brain, but it makes no phenomenal difference. Then the distinctive contribution arriving at such solutions might make to your welfare seems to go missing in this case.

Suppose that all phenomenal states are sensory states. Then there is a problem just like the one about a priori justification. We'd find ourselves with the following commitments: events in your intellectual life make a contribution to your welfare that is not constituted by sensory experience, but it is constituted by some experience, and all experiences are sensory experiences. Again, something has to give.

Some philosophers will reject the connection between value and phenomenology. Plausibly, at least some values do not constitutively depend on experience. So maybe the values realized by events in your intellectual life are always like these. Other philosophers will reject the axiological autonomy of our intellectual life. They might embrace some form of hedonism according to which all value derives from pleasant sensations. On this view, solving a logical puzzle might be valuable because it releases tension. But another option is to challenge the view that all phenomenal states are sensory states. Figuring out to what extent this is workable requires getting clearer about cognitive phenomenology. Hence there is some motivation from value theory to pursue such a project.

Semantics. Suppose you take your child to the zoo for the first time. You stand in front of the lion cage and say, "Those are lions." Your child sees the lions. Though she never heard of lions before, now that she is acquainted with them she can entertain various thoughts about lions. You move on to the tiger cage and say, "Those are tigers." Your child sees the tigers. Though she never heard of tigers before, now that she is acquainted with them she can entertain various thoughts about tigers. Suppose you move on to the bear cage and say, "Those are bears." This time, however, something prevents your demonstration from making any phenomenal difference to your child's experience. Given that she never heard of bears before, even though visually detected information about bears is represented somehow in her brain, she still cannot entertain thoughts about bears. If there is no difference in phenomenology, then there is no difference in what your child can think about.

Now compare thoughts about simple abstract matters such as addition, subtraction, and multiplication. Just as with lions, tigers, and bears, at some point in our lives we gain abilities to think about addition, subtraction, and multiplication. Further, it seems, just as with the animals, we gain these abilities to think about the operations through episodes of discovery or instruction.

There are two claims it is tempting to make about the episodes of discovery or instruction that enable thoughts about simple abstract matters. They parallel the claims we considered when looking at connections to epistemology and value theory. So first, there is the claim that in one way these episodes are different from the episodes that enable thoughts about sensible subject matter: they are constitutively independent of sensory experience. Maybe you learn about addition by manipulating collections. But the sensory experiences seem both inessential to and insufficient for acquainting you with addition itself. At most, perhaps, they are parts of a larger episode that connects your thought to addition. Second, there is a similarity between the episodes grounding thoughts about simple abstract matters and episodes grounding thoughts about sensible subject matter. In particular, both are connected to phenomenology. Because bears remain phenomenally invisible for your daughter, she cannot think about or at least cannot think certain kinds of thoughts about bears. Similarly, if addition remains phenomenally invisible to you, then you cannot think about or at least cannot think certain kinds of thoughts about addition.

The rest of the story can be anticipated. Suppose all phenomenal states are sensory states. This raises a problem, for then we'd find ourselves with the following commitments: certain episodes of discovery or learning that enable you to think about simple abstract matters are constitutively independent of sensory experience, but they are constitutively dependent on some experience, and all experiences are sensory experiences. These can't all be true.

Some philosophers will reject the connection between thought and phenomenology, at least for the case of simple abstract matters. Consider logical operations. It seems we just find ourselves thinking thoughts in which we discern logical form, but it does not seem that this depends on experiencing logical operations. Maybe thoughts about arithmetical operations are similar. Other philosophers will reject the idea that thought about abstract matters is constitutively independent of sensory states. One possibility is that both thoughts about sensible subject matter and thoughts about abstract subject matter depend on sensory phenomenology, and the differences between them are constituted by non-phenomenal factors. But another option is to challenge the view that all phenomenal states are sensory states. Figuring out to what extent this is workable requires getting clearer about cognitive phenomenology. Hence there is some motivation from semantics to pursue such a project.

Finally, aside from its connection to other topics, one might find the topic of cognitive phenomenology interesting in itself. The very fact that there could be debate about it is puzzling. One might think that if cognitive states are phenomenally different from sensory states, then this should be obvious to anyone who has had both conscious cognitive states and conscious sensory states. But it turns out that this is not the case. There is room for reasonable disagreement about the status of cognitive phenomenology, and this suggests there is a fine structure underlying the issue that needs uncovering. We will begin this excavation process in the next section.

Terms

Recall the example of seeing from above:

[Seeing] You are looking for your dogs in the dog park. At first you cannot pick them out of the mass of other dogs. But then you see them there chasing a tennis ball.

There are at least four different things we might say about this case.

First, it is a change in mental state. I will not try to say what a mental state is in more basic terms. I will take it as a primitive. One might say that a mental state consists of a subject instantiating a mental property. That is a possible characterization in more basic terms – so long as the notions of subject and mental property are taken to be more basic than the notion of a mental state. One might, however, think that the notion of a mental state is more basic than the notion of a subject. Perhaps what it is for there to be a subject is for there to be an appropriately related bundle of mental states. Nothing in this book will hinge on taking a stance on this issue.

In chapter 4 the difference between mental states and mental events will matter, and I will say something about the difference between them then. Outside of chapter 4, however, I will use the term "mental state" to cover both.

Talk about mental states can be construed in two ways. There are mental state types and there are mental state tokens. Suppose you see your dogs and your friend sees your dogs. Then in one sense you and your friend are in the same mental state: you both see your dogs. This is a mental state type. In another sense, however, you and your friend are in different mental states: there is the instance of the mental state of seeing your dogs that occurs in you and there is the instance of the mental state of seeing your dogs that occurs in your friend. These are mental state tokens. In general when I talk about mental states – and mental events – without qualification I intend to refer to mental state types. If I want to refer to mental state tokens I will make this explicit.

The second thing we might say about [Seeing] is that it is a change in phenomenal state. By a phenomenal state I mean a mental state that is individuated by what it is like for one to be in it. What it is like for one to be in a mental state is that mental state's phenomenal character. And to say that its phenomenal character individuates a mental state is to say that there is nothing more and nothing less required for being in that very mental state than being in a mental state with just the same phenomenal character.

So if a mental state is a phenomenal state, then there is some particular phenomenal character and it is both necessary and sufficient for one to be in that state that one is in a state with that phenomenal character. This gives us a definition of phenomenal states in terms of the notions of mental state and phenomenal character: a mental state M is a phenomenal state just in case there is a phenomenal character such that being in M is being in a mental state with that phenomenal character. When you see your dogs they look some specific way to you. You are in a visual state with a particular phenomenal character. The state of being in a mental state with just that phenomenal character is a phenomenal state.

In addition to the notion of a mental state that is individuated by its phenomenal character, it is useful to have a notion of a mental state that essentially has some phenomenal character or other, perhaps within a certain restricted range, but that is not individuated by any particular phenomenal character. I will call such states phenomenally conscious mental states.[2]

The third thing we might say about [Seeing] is that there is a change in phenomenally conscious state. On any particular occasion when you see your dogs they look some specific way. But just what way will differ on different occasions. For example, you might see your dogs from their front, back, or side. In each case there is some way your dogs look to you. But the exact way they look to you differs from case to case. Still, in each case you do count as being in the mental state of seeing your dogs. So the state of seeing your dogs is not a phenomenal state. It is an example of a phenomenally conscious state.

Plausibly if one is in a mental state with some phenomenal character, then there is some phenomenal state one is in – the one individuated by just that phenomenal character. So we might define phenomenally conscious states in terms of phenomenal states like this: a mental state M is a phenomenally conscious state just in case necessarily, if one is in M, then because one is in M there is some phenomenal state P such that one is in P.

It is worth saying something about the motivation for including the "because" in this definition. Suppose we dropped it and opted for the following alternative: a mental state M is a phenomenally conscious state just in case necessarily, if one is in M, then there is some phenomenal state P such that one is in P. Now consider the conjunctive state of seeing your dogs and being such that Socrates is mortal. Necessarily if one is in this conjunctive state, then there is some phenomenal state one is in. But plausibly the conjunctive state is not a phenomenally conscious state. It is a state that partly consists in a phenomenally conscious state – the conjunct in which you see your dogs, not the conjunct in which you are such that Socrates is mortal.

The addition of "because" fixes this problem. "Because" introduces an explanatory context and explanation is more discriminating than necessitation. The relevant form of explanation is non-causal, and aside from "because" it is typically picked out by "grounds" or "in virtue of." It will figure prominently in this book.

To get a clearer view of this form of explanation, contrast (A) with (B):

(A) My car is illegally parked because I was in a rush this morning.
(B) My car is illegally parked because it is parked next to a fire hydrant and parking next to a fire hydrant is illegal.

Statement (A) gives a causal explanation. The fact that I was in a rush this morning causally explains the fact that my car is parked illegally. Statement (B) gives a non-causal explanation. The facts that my car is parked next to a fire hydrant and parking next to a fire hydrant is illegal do not causally explain the fact that my car is parked illegally. Still, they do stand in some explanatory relation to it. They tell us what facts ground the fact that my car is illegally parked. They are the facts in virtue of which my car is illegally parked.

To see that this form of explanation is different from necessitation contrast (B) with (C):

(C) Necessarily, if my car is parked next to a fire hydrant and parking next to a fire hydrant is illegal, then my car is illegally parked.

Both (B) and (C) are true. From (C), however, we can infer (C*):

(C*) Necessarily, if my car is parked next to a fire hydrant and parking next to a fire hydrant is illegal and Socrates is mortal, then my car is illegally parked.

It would be silly to say something like (C*), but (C*) is true, and its truth follows from the truth of (C). Contrast (B*):

(B*) My car is illegally parked because it is parked next to a fire hydrant and parking next to a fire hydrant is illegal and Socrates is mortal.

(B*) is not just silly; it is false, and it does not follow from (B). This is a difference with respect to what is called monotonicity. Necessitation is monotonic. That means that from X necessitates Y it follows that for any Z, X and Z also necessitate Y. Grounding is non-monotonic. That means that from X grounds Y it does not follow that for any Z, X and Z also ground Y. The reason for this difference is that necessitation is not an explanatory notion, and so is not constrained by any relation of explanatory relevance, but grounding is an explanatory notion, and so is constrained by a relation of explanatory relevance. The problem with (B*) is this: the fact that Socrates is mortal is explanatorily irrelevant to the fact that my car is illegally parked.

Similarly, when you see your dogs, the fact that Socrates is mortal is explanatorily irrelevant to the fact that you are in a phenomenal state. So the conjunctive state of seeing your dogs and being such that Socrates is mortal does not ground the fact that you are in a phenomenal state. It follows that while seeing your dogs is phenomenally conscious, the conjunctive state of seeing your dogs and being such that Socrates is mortal is not phenomenally conscious, according to the characterization of phenomenally conscious state adopted here.

Aside from being explanatory and so non-monotonic, I will assume that grounding – at least as it figures in this book – has three other properties: it is irreflexive (X does not ground X), transitive (if X grounds Y, and Y grounds Z, then X grounds Z), and necessitating (if X grounds Y, then X necessitates Y). It is controversial whether grounding as such has all of these properties, and I am not claiming that it does. What I am claiming is that there is at least some form of the grounding relation – a restriction on the general grounding relation – that does have all of these properties and it is this notion that figures in the theses with which I am concerned.[3]

The fourth thing we might say about [Seeing] is that it is a change in sensory state, rather than, or at least in addition to, a change in cognitive state. This distinction between sensory and cognitive states is central to the book. It is worth exploring it in some detail.

Before getting into those details, however, I want to flag two simplifying assumptions about mental states that I will make, at least provisionally. First: every mental state is either sensory or cognitive. Some might be both. But every mental state is at least one or the other. Second: every token mental state has some representational content. I will discuss the notion of having content at some length in chapter 6. For now I will presuppose some intuitive grasp of it as that aspect of mental states that makes them about or directed at the world. The second simplifying assumption I am making is that every token mental state has such an aspect. If you think it is implausible that every mental state has some representational content when tokened and is at least sensory or cognitive, then just interpret my usage of "mental state" as a restricted one that only applies to those states that satisfy the assumptions.

With these preliminaries out of the way, let us contrast the following two mental states: thinking that there is mail in your mailbox, seeing that there is mail in your mailbox.

One obvious difference between thinking that there is mail in your mailbox and seeing that there is mail in your mailbox is that you can do the former but not the latter with your eyes closed. Visual perceptions occur because of events in eyes. Olfactory experiences occur because of events in noses. More generally sensory perceptions occur because of events in a finite stock of sensory receptors. Perhaps it is possible to enumerate some list of causes and say that a mental state is a sensory state just in case it is caused in one of these ways and cognitive otherwise.

I have two worries about this approach. First, it is not clear that the list of causes of sensory states is enumerable. It is enumerable if we consider actual creatures, since there is a finite number of them. But if we consider possible creatures as well, and I think we should, then it is not clear why we should think the list of causes of sensory states is enumerable. Second, the consideration of possible creatures suggests this approach is backwards. Imagine some possible creature, maybe a basilisk. Why should some events that happen in it count as causes of its sensory states and some not? It seems that in answering this question we must appeal to a non-etiological understanding of sensory states.

One possible non-etiological difference between sensory states and cognitive states is in their representational contents. Perhaps sensory states can only have contents of a certain kind – e.g. non-conceptual contents. And perhaps cognitive states can only have contents of another kind – e.g. conceptual contents. These claims are controversial however. Some philosophers argue that sensory states can have conceptual contents.[4] Other philosophers argue that cognitive states can have non-conceptual contents.[5] Whatever one makes of these debates it seems that the distinction between sensory and cognitive states is something obvious and that we should be able to characterize it independently of taking a stand on them.

Another related approach focuses on which properties sensory states and cognitive states represent. Perhaps sensory states can only represent certain "low-level" properties – e.g. shapes, colors, sounds, smells, etc. And perhaps cognitive states are different in that they can represent "high-level" properties – e.g. meanings, natural kinds, artifactual kinds, and causal relations. These claims are also controversial. Some philosophers argue that sensory states can represent high-level properties.[6] When you see that there is mail in your mailbox, for example, it is natural to think that you have a visual experience that represents the properties of being mail and being a mailbox. These are artifactual kinds. Once again, however, whatever one makes of this debate it seems that the distinction between sensory and cognitive states is something obvious and that we should be able to characterize independently of taking a stand on it.

Let us suppose that the mental states of thinking that there is mail in your mailbox and seeing that there is mail in your mailbox have some common representational content – something common picked out by the clause "that there is mail in your mailbox." Still there is a clear difference between the mental states: when you see that there is mail in your mailbox the mail seems to be sitting there before you. You both represent that there is mail in your mailbox and are aware of the parts of your immediate environment that make it true that there is mail in your mailbox. The content of the sensory state is tied to what seems present here and now. This need not be so when you think that there is mail in your mailbox. You might very well think that there is mail in your mailbox when you are miles away from your mailbox. The content of the cognitive state is free from what seems present here and now. In my view this observation is the key to drawing the distinction between sensory and cognitive states. Transforming it into a clear and adequately general characterization of the distinction between sensory and cognitive states will take some work however.

It will prove useful to start by saying something about two notions. The first notion is that of awareness. Awareness is a two-place determinable relation between a subject and an object. It is determinable because there are different ways a subject can be aware of an object. Two examples are seeing and hearing. Seeing a fire truck is a way of being aware of it. Hearing a fire truck is another way of being aware of it. What makes these forms of awareness? As I will understand awareness, the answer is threefold.

First, seeing a fire truck and hearing a fire truck both enable you to entertain demonstrative thoughts about the fire truck. When you see or hear the fire truck you are thereby enabled to entertain thoughts of the form, "that is red" or "that is loud," where "that" demonstratively refers to the fire truck. In general states of awareness enable demonstrative thoughts about objects of awareness – at least in creatures with the general capacity to entertain demonstrative thoughts at all.[7]

Second, seeing a fire truck and hearing a fire truck both phenomenally differentiate the fire truck from other things. Say you are in the Sonoran Desert staring at your feet. You just see your feet standing out from some sand. Unbeknownst to you there is a flat-tailed horned lizard next to your left foot. You don't know that it is there because you cannot see it. And you cannot see it because it is has camouflaged itself. It is playing a role along with the sand and your feet in causing you to have a visual experience with a certain phenomenal character. But that is not enough for it to be an object of visual awareness. What more is required is for your visual phenomenology to be so structured that the lizard stands out from its environment, so that it is no longer camouflaged. In general states of awareness phenomenally differentiate objects of awareness from other things.[8]

Third and finally, the two features are connected. If seeing the fire truck didn't phenomenally differentiate the fire truck from other things, then it wouldn't enable demonstrative thoughts about the fire truck. A similar point holds for hearing the fire truck. In general states of awareness enable demonstrative thoughts about objects of awareness, at least in part because they phenomenally differentiate objects of awareness.

The second notion that will help us in characterizing the distinction between sensory and cognitive states is the notion of what I will call an environmental witness to a proposition. Consider two ways of seeing that there is mail in your mailbox. The first way is to look inside the mailbox and observe the mail there. In this case you are visually aware of the part of your environment that makes it true that there is mail in your mailbox. The second way is to look at your mailbox from a distance and observe the mail carrier standing in front of it, doing something that could only be putting mail in your mailbox, and then walking away. In this case you are not visually aware of the part of your environment that makes it true that there is mail in your mailbox. Rather, you are visually aware of indicators in your environment that suggest there is mail in your mailbox. Often we count as perceiving that something is the case even though we are not aware of the part of the environment that makes it the case but only indicators in our immediate environment that suggest it is the case. So there are truth-makers for propositions and there are truth-indicators for propositions. I will use the term "witness to a proposition" to cover both. An environmental witness to a proposition is a witness to that proposition that is located in one's spatiotemporal vicinity.

When you think that there is mail in your mailbox you represent that there is mail in your mailbox in a way that is independent of current awareness of an environmental witness to that proposition. This characterization gives some structure to the commonsensical idea that thought is free from what seems present here and now. When you see that there is mail in your mailbox — by seeing the mail or by seeing the activity of the mail carrier — you represent that there is mail in your mailbox in a way that is dependent on current awareness of an environmental witness to that proposition. This characterization gives some structure to the commonsensical idea that sensation is tied to what seems present here and now.

The foregoing discussion of the particular mental states of thinking that there is mail in your mailbox and seeing that there is mail in your mailbox suggests the following general notions: a mental state represents that p in a cognitive way just in case it represents that p in a way that is independent of current awareness of an environmental witness to p; a mental state represents that p in a sensory way just in case it represents that p in a way that is dependent on current awareness of an environmental witness to p. I think these notions of sensory and cognitive ways of representing a proposition are useful, but in order to formulate an adequately general characterization of the distinction between sensory and cognitive states in terms of them we need to introduce some minor adjustments.

Consider the following experiences: visually hallucinating that there is mail in your mailbox; visually recollecting mail in your mailbox; visually imagining mail in your mailbox; feeling the thrill of finding mail in your mailbox; feeling your heartbeat speed up as you approach your mailbox. Hallucinations, recollections, imaginings, emotions, and bodily sensations should all count as sensory states in the broad sense that is relevant to debates about cognitive phenomenology.[9] But awareness of environmental witnesses to propositions does not figure in any of them. Even so, states akin to such awareness do: in hallucination there is seeming awareness of one's environment; in recollection and imagination there is recollected and imagined awareness of one's environment; emotions color awareness of one's environment; and bodily sensations involve awareness of one's body which we might count as a limiting case of one's environment. So here is how we might define appropriately adjusted notions of sensory and cognitive ways of representing a proposition: a mental state M represents that p in a sensory way just in case M represents that p in a way that is dependent on current awareness of an environmental witness to p or a state that is akin to such awareness; a mental state M represents that p in a cognitive way just in case M represents that p in a way that is independent of current awareness of an environmental witness to p or a state that is akin to such awareness.

Consider the mental state of seeing mail in your mailbox and hoping it is your paycheck. This mental state illustrates two features of the notions of sensory and cognitive ways of representing a proposition. First, a mental state might represent in both sensory and cognitive ways. Indeed a mental state might represent the very same proposition in both sensory and cognitive ways: maybe you both see and think that there is mail in your mailbox at the same time. One proposition, two ways of representing it. Second, awareness of one's environment might enable one to be in a mental state that does not depend on continuation of that awareness. When you hope that some seen mail includes your paycheck, for example, your hope refers to that particular mail because it is the mail that you see. So your visual awareness enables you to have that hope. But the hope might persist beyond the visual awareness: you can still have the hope after closing your eyes. So the hope does not depend on current awareness of the mail.

Now we have characterizations of sensory and cognitive ways of representing a proposition. It is easy to formulate characterizations of sensory and cognitive states in terms of them. As already illustrated, however, really there are four relevant notions. A mental state M is partly sensory just in case M represents part of its content in a sensory way. A mental state M is wholly sensory just in case M represents all of its content in a sensory way. A mental state M is partly cognitive just in case M represents part of its content in a cognitive way. A mental state M is wholly cognitive just in case M represents all of its content in a cognitive way.

Theses

Recall the example of intuiting from above:

> [Intuiting] In a book you read, "If $a < 1$, then $2 - 2a > 0$," and you wonder whether this is true. Then you "see" how a's being less than 1 makes $2a$ smaller than 2 and so $2 - 2a$ greater than 0.

There is a change in cognitive state and there is a change in phenomenal state. Plausibly the change in phenomenal state is somehow due to the change in cognitive state. But this does not show that proponents of cognitive phenomenology are right and opponents of cognitive phenomenology are wrong. Proponents of cognitive phenomenology are committed to a specific thesis that should be distinguished from other nearby theses – some weaker, some stronger, and some orthogonal.[10]

The specific thesis that proponents of cognitive phenomenology endorse implies that some cognitive states make phenomenal differences that are irreducible to those made by sensory states. There are new phenomenal states in addition to wholly sensory phenomenal states. Let us adopt the following official formulation of this view:

> Irreducibility: Some cognitive states put one in phenomenal states for which no wholly sensory states suffice.

The idea of a cognitive state putting one in a phenomenal state implicitly invokes the "because" relation again. We can make this explicit with a more cumbersome formulation of Irreducibility: Some cognitive states are such that because one is in them one is in a phenomenal state for which no wholly sensory state suffices. In general when I use locutions such as "put one in" and "make" as in "make a phenomenal difference" I have this sort of interpretation in mind.

In saying that a phenomenal state is one for which no wholly sensory state suffices I mean that no wholly sensory state necessitates that one is in that phenomenal state. And it follows that no wholly sensory state puts one in that phenomenal state – in the sense just highlighted. This is compatible with a sensory state causing one to be in that phenomenal state on some occasion.

One will find different authors calling phenomenal states for which Irreducibility holds either cognitive phenomenal states, or cognitive qualia, or just cognitive phenomenology. But usage isn't standardized. I will call them cognitive phenomenal states. If a phenomenal state is such that some wholly sensory states suffice for being in it, then I will call that phenomenal state a sensory phenomenal state.

So suppose you intuit that if $a < 1$, then $2 - 2a > 0$. In doing so you might say to yourself, "If $a < 1$, then $2 - 2a > 0$," or you might visualize the variable "a" or the numeral "1," or might experience kinesthetic sensations as you think of the quantity assigned to "$2a$" shrinking. These are all sensory phenomenal states. If you believe Irreducibility and you think this case of intuiting is an example of irreducible cognitive phenomenology, then you believe that even taken all together these sensory phenomenal states fail to make the very same phenomenal difference intuiting that if $a < 1$, then $2 - 2a > 0$ makes to your overall experience. There is some phenomenal state left over which only the cognitive state of intuiting that if $a < 1$, then $2 - 2a > 0$ – or maybe a cognitive state very similar to this one – can put you in. This is what it is to believe in cognitive phenomenal states.

Now let us consider a thesis that falls short of Irreducibility. This is the thesis that some cognitive states make phenomenal differences. Unlike Irreducibility this thesis does not add that the phenomenal differences are irreducible to those made by sensory states. Let us adopt the following official formulation of this weaker thesis:

Phenomenal Presence: Some cognitive states put one in phenomenal states.

The thesis of Phenomenal Presence is equivalent to the thesis that some cognitive states are phenomenally conscious. Recall that a mental state is phenomenally conscious just in case if one is in it then it puts one in some phenomenal state or other. Phenomenal Presence implies that some cognitive states are phenomenally conscious in this sense. What it doesn't imply is that the phenomenal states such cognitive states put one in are any different from the sorts of phenomenal states sensory states put one in.

Suppose you think that whenever one intuits that $a < 1$, then $2 - 2a > 0$ then one is thereby put in some phenomenal state or other. But suppose you think that these phenomenal states are just those involved in visualizing the variable "a" or the numeral "1," or those involved in experiencing kinesthetic sensations as you think of the quantity assigned to "$2a$" shrinking. If this is your view then you think that the intuition is phenomenally present – it makes some phenomenal difference whenever it occurs – but that it does not introduce any new phenomenal states distinct from those that various wholly sensory states might put one in. This view falls short of commitment to irreducible cognitive phenomenology.

Now let us consider a thesis that goes beyond Irreducibility. This is the thesis that some cognitive states make phenomenal differences that are independent of those made by sensory states. Independence is a modal notion: it has to do with what is possible. Two things are independent if they can exist with or without each other – i.e. the existence of one neither includes nor excludes the existence of the other. Let us adopt the following official formulation of this independence thesis:

Independence: Some cognitive states put one in phenomenal states that are independent of sensory states.

Independence is stronger than Irreducibility. That is, Independence entails Irreducibility but Irreducibility does not entail Independence. To see that Independence entails Irreducibility suppose some phenomenal state P is independent of sensory states. Then being in wholly sensory states does not imply – i.e. suffice for – being in P. To see that Irreducibility does not entail Independence consider a cognitive phenomenal state P that is also partly sensory. Being in wholly sensory states does not suffice for being in P, but one cannot be in P without being in some sensory state.

If you endorse Irreducibility then you think there are cognitive phenomenal states. These are phenomenal states for which wholly sensory states do not suffice. If you endorse Independence then you think there are what we might call purely cognitive phenomenal states. These are phenomenal states for which wholly cognitive states do suffice. If one endorses Irreducibility but rejects Independence then one thinks that even though there are phenomenal states for which wholly sensory states do not suffice, there are no phenomenal states for which wholly cognitive states do suffice. On this view whenever one is in a phenomenal state it is at least in part because one is in a sensory state.

Now let us consider a thesis that is orthogonal to Irreducibility. The literature on cognitive phenomenology intersects with the literature on what is called phenomenal intentionality. Proponents of cognitive phenomenology tend to propound phenomenal intentionality as well. The basic idea of phenomenal intentionality is that for some token mental states their phenomenal characters determine their representational contents. Let us adopt the following formulation of this thesis:

Phenomenal Intentionality: Some phenomenal states determine intentional states.

Here I am using "intentional" and "representational" equivalently: so an alternative formulation is that some phenomenal states determine representational states – i.e. states with representational content. Phenomenal Intentionality goes beyond the provisional assumption that every token mental state has representational content, since it implies that every token of the same phenomenal state has the same representational content.

As I have formulated it, Phenomenal Intentionality leaves open exactly how to understand the determination relation it says phenomenal states bear to intentional states. One option is to think of determination as necessitation. Another option is to think of determination as grounding. I will take Phenomenal Intentionality to be the general thesis, which can be made more precise in light of further reflection.

Irreducibility and Phenomenal Intentionality are related but orthogonal. They are orthogonal because there are no logical entailment relations in either direction. It is logically consistent to endorse Irreducibility and reject Phenomenal Intentionality and it is logically consistent to endorse Phenomenal Intentionality and reject Irreducibility. The two theses are related, however, because there are grounds for thinking that the sorts of phenomenal states for which Irreducibility holds (i.e. cognitive phenomenal states) are ones for which Phenomenal Intentionality holds (i.e. such that they determine intentional states). This is why proponents of cognitive phenomenology tend to propound Phenomenal Intentionality.

In fact proponents of cognitive phenomenology tend to propound a more specific thesis, namely:

Cognitive Phenomenal Intentionality: Some phenomenal states determine cognitive intentional states.

This thesis is not orthogonal to Irreducibility: it is stronger than Irreducibility. That is, Cognitive Phenomenal Intentionality logically entails Irreducibility, but Irreducibility does not logically entail Cognitive Phenomenal Intentionality. To see that Cognitive Phenomenal Intentionality logically entails Irreducibility suppose some phenomenal state P determines a cognitive intentional state. Then being in a wholly sensory state does not suffice for being in P, because once you are in P you are thereby in some cognitive state and so not in a wholly sensory state. To see that Irreducibility does not logically entail Cognitive Phenomenal Intentionality suppose there are phenomenal states for which wholly sensory states do not suffice but which themselves do not suffice for cognitive states. Maybe these are a kind of cognitive "raw feel." One might think no such phenomenal states exist, but this is a substantive issue that goes beyond purely logical reasoning.

So there are four theses to be distinguished: Irreducibility, Phenomenal Presence, Independence, and Cognitive Phenomenal Intentionality. I see Irreducibility as the main issue in the debate about cognitive phenomenology. Proponents accept it; opponents reject it. But much of philosophical interest emerges from considering its connections to the other theses, so these lie within the scope of our inquiry as well.

Notes

1 For similar discussions of the significance of cognitive phenomenology see Siewert 1998, 2013, Smithies 2013a, and Strawson 2011.
2 See Siegel 2010.
3 For more on grounding see Correia and Schnieder 2012, Rosen 2010, Schaffer 2009, Sider 2011, and Trogdon 2013.
4 See, for example, McDowell 1994.
5 See, for example, Beck 2012.
6 See, for example, Siegel 2006c, 2010.

7 For further discussion of this feature of awareness see Snowdon 1990, Siegel 2006b, and Tye 2009.

8 For further discussion of this feature of awareness see Dretske 1969 and Siegel 2006a.

9 See Lormand 1996 and Tye and Wright 2011.

10 See Smithies 2013b. I put things somewhat differently, but our interpretations of the issues are in agreement.

1

INTROSPECTION

Disputes about cognitive phenomenology are disputes about our conscious mental life. Much of our knowledge of our conscious mental life derives from introspection. A natural idea, then, is to try to settle the disputes about cognitive phenomenology by appeals to introspection.

This natural idea, however, turns out to be problematic. Do phenomenally conscious thoughts inherit their phenomenal characters from concurrent sensory states? Consider two appeals to introspection in the literature that address this question:

> Striking examples of thoughts occurring, conscious, but in the absence of verbal expression or imagery, are to be found where there is what we might call an abrupt shift in the direction of thought. Suppose you are sitting and reading one morning, and suddenly you remember some incipient appointment – you wonder when exactly it was, feel anxious that you may have missed it, and look at your watch. The thought of the appointment and when it was is an occurrence of consciousness, but it may not be verbalized silently or aloud. You may not have said to yourself – "I have an appointment around now, don't I? When was it? Did I miss it?" You may not even have said something fragmentary like: "Appointment!

When? Miss it?" And you may not have visualized or imaged any item or event at the time of this thought, such as the person with whom you had the appointment, or the place at which you were to meet. But this little wordless episode of noniconic thinking – your suddenly realizing that you had an appointment – is phenomenally conscious, and the way it seems to you to have this thought differs from the way it would seem to you to have imagery experience of some sort.[1]

From a phenomenological perspective, thinking a thought is much like running a sentence through one's head and/or (in some cases) having a mental image in mind together with (in some cases) an emotional/bodily response and a feeling of effort if the thought is complex or difficult to grasp. For example, when you think that claret is delightful, you may have an experience of sub-vocalized speech (saying to yourself "Claret is delightful"), or you may bring mental images of claret to mind, or perhaps even remember occasions where you had a particularly delightful claret. Further, a feeling of warmth may descend upon you, along with a smile on your lips with an associated facial sensation. The only phenomenology to be found when a thought is introspected is the phenomenology of these and other such states.[2]

The appeals are before us, but it isn't really clear what to think in light of them. Some readers might sympathize with the first, remembering similar examples from their own life. Other readers might do the same with the second. Opinion divides. Now what?

The first section below is about the role introspection should play in disputes about cognitive phenomenology. There are two extreme views: introspective evidence should settle them directly; introspective evidence should be ignored completely. Between these there are any number of intermediate views. I will suggest that some intermediate view is true, but that it is difficult to say anything very precise about the role introspection should play in advance of assessing various arguments that appeal to it in some way or another.

The balance of the chapter is dedicated to one such argumentative strategy. The strategy is to draw conclusions about cognitive phenomenology from premises about the kind of introspective access we have to our conscious thoughts. David Pitt has developed the most detailed argument of this sort. In the second section ("The Argument from Introspectability"), I explain Pitt's argument. In the third section ("Assessing the Argument from Introspectability"), I discuss challenges to it.

The role of introspection

Some things we can tell by introspection.

I can tell by introspection that it looks to me as if there is a computer in front of me. I can tell by introspection that it does not look to me as if there is an elephant in front of me. In general I have some introspective knowledge of what phenomenally conscious states I am in.

Suppose I feel an itch in my ear and a pinch on my elbow. Aside from being able to tell by introspection that I feel these things, I can also tell by introspection that the itch feels different from the pinch. Suppose I also feel a tickle on my shoulder. Plausibly, if I'm attentive enough, I can also tell by introspection whether the tickle is phenomenally more similar to the itch than it is to the pinch. In general I have some introspective knowledge about the phenomenal similarities and differences among the phenomenally conscious states I am in.

Say I have a headache and it is distracting me from other business. Dwelling on the headache I might ask myself, "Is it a sharp headache or a dull headache?" And presumably I can tell by introspection how well the candidate descriptions fit my headache. If the headache is sharp, I know that it is sharp and I know that it is not dull. In general I have some introspective knowledge about the accuracy of some simple descriptions of phenomenally conscious states I am in.

At this point it is natural to ask: what is the nature of this introspective capacity that reveals such facts about presence and absence, similarity and difference, accuracy and inaccuracy?

This is a difficult question, and there are many different approaches to it in the literature. One might worry that it is impossible to pursue our present inquiry – about the proper role of introspection in exploring cognitive phenomenology – without first saying something about the nature of introspection. For its nature will determine its proper role. Consider vision, however. You do not need to know much about the nature of vision to know that you shouldn't try to determine the sound of an instrument by looking at it. Simple observation and reflection suffice. Similarly, I believe we can establish some useful guidelines about the role introspection might play in our inquiry without committing to a specific theory about its nature. So for now I will bracket the question about its nature. It will come up again below.

The examples catalogued above illustrate what I have in mind by introspection. Our question is: how might the capacity illustrated in them be used to settle disputes about cognitive phenomenology? Let us focus on Irreducibility and consider two extreme views:

> Extreme Optimism: Introspection alone can put us in a position to know whether Irreducibility is true.

> Extreme Pessimism: Introspection cannot make any difference to our position to know whether Irreducibility is true.

To my knowledge, no one endorses either view. Siewert and Tye and Wright, for example, do not just stop with their introspective reports. They supplement those reports with further argumentation. And skeptics about introspection generally allow that our introspective reports at least form a data set that can be drawn on in theorizing about the mind. Still, I believe that Extreme Optimism and Extreme Pessimism are useful focal points: examining reasons for rejecting them will not serve any ad hominem purpose, but it will bring to light considerations relevant to developing a more nuanced view about the role introspection should play in our inquiry.

The picture suggested by Extreme Optimism is that just as you can tell by introspection whether you are having a headache, or whether it feels different from the itch on your ear, or whether it is sharp, you can tell by introspection whether Irreducibility is true – i.e. whether some cognitive states put one in phenomenal states for which no wholly sensory states suffice. On its face this seems incredible. Suppose you can tell the following by introspection: that you are thinking about dinner, that your thought and your hunger are phenomenally different, and that your thought is intruding on the course of more lofty philosophical reflections. None of this suggests you can tell whether Irreducibility is true by introspection. Irreducibility is a (i) logically complex (ii) generalization about (iii) possible (iv) explanatory relations. The claims we typically know by introspection are (a) logically simple claims about the (b) actual (c) intrinsic properties of (d) particular mental states. So there are these four differences – (i) instead of (a); (ii) instead of (d); (iii) instead of (b); and (iv) instead of (c) – that distinguish Irreducibility from the claims with respect to which introspection generally inspires confidence.

Consider also the fact that even after introspecting philosophers disagree about Irreducibility. Why is there such disagreement? Bayne and Spener helpfully distinguish four candidate explanations.[3]

First, two philosophers might disagree because there are individual differences between them. Some philosophers have irreducibly cognitive phenomenal states and some do not. Those that have them introspect their irreducibility. Those that do not have them do not introspect their irreducibility. Hence the disagreement. The disputants are correct in their introspective judgments about themselves – but they go wrong in generalizing to others.

Second, two philosophers might disagree because there are terminological variations between them. The term "phenomenal state" is often introduced using sensory examples – itches, bodily sensations, visual perceptions, and the like. Suppose one disputant assigns a meaning to "phenomenal state" according to which a mental state is a phenomenal state just in case it is phenomenally similar to itches, bodily sensations, visual perceptions, and the like. Suppose the other disputant assigns a meaning to "phenomenal state" according to which a mental state is a phenomenal state just in case it is individuated by what it is like for one to be in it – where the locution "what it is like" is not itself tied to the sensory.[4] Then both disputants might sometimes be in what I have been calling cognitive phenomenal states, but only the second will agree to call them that. In this case the disputants are not making introspective errors; rather they are engaging in a verbal dispute.

Third, two philosophers might disagree because they have different background beliefs and expectations. The interaction between observations and background beliefs and expectations is a complicated matter. Here is a simple perceptual example illustrating the phenomenon. Suppose Al is confident that all swans are white, and subscribes to an elaborate but mistaken theory that implies that all swans must be white. Suppose Beth does not subscribe to this theory, but has only ever observed white swans, and so tentatively believes all swans are white but is open to changing her view. Then both Al and Beth see a black swan. On the basis of this observation Al comes to believe that there are birds that could easily trick the naive observer into thinking there are black swans, but that are really of a different species. Beth comes to believe there are black swans. Perhaps something similar is going on with disputes about cognitive phenomenology. Any such explanation of the disagreement will require an elaboration of the relevant background beliefs and expectations and a story about how they might interact with introspective observations. There is no a priori reason to rule out such an explanation however.

Fourth, two philosophers might disagree because introspection is insufficient to settle the question of whether Irreducibility is true. This is a result of what Bayne and Spener call operational constraints. Here is a simple perceptual example illustrating the phenomenon. Suppose Al and Beth wonder what is inside an opaque box. They each have different conjectures. Suppose, further, that the only data they rely on in determining which conjecture is correct is what they can tell by looking at the box. It would be no surprise if Al and Beth fail to come to an agreement. Visual perception does not enable one to tell what is inside opaque containers. It just does not work like that. Maybe there are similar operational constraints on introspection. Introspection will tell you whether you are thinking about dinner, whether your thought and your hunger are phenomenally different, and whether your thought is intruding on the course of more lofty philosophical reflections. But it will not tell you whether Irreducibility is true. If this is so, then Extreme Optimism is false.

It is reasonable to suppose that there are at least some individual differences, terminological variations, and differences in background beliefs and expectations among philosophers. And it is reasonable to suppose that these do contribute somewhat toward sustaining disagreement about Irreducibility. I doubt that they constitute the whole story though. Operational constraints are at least part – and probably a large part – of the story as well. Further, the applicability of this form of explanation to the disagreement about Irreducibility is a typical instance of a general phenomenon, sometimes exhibited by introspection with respect to other disputes about the mental and sometimes exhibited by other basic sources of knowledge with respect to various disputes about their own domains. Before trying to characterize the general phenomenon, let us consider some examples.

The following are disputed claims about mental states, observable properties, and abstract objects:

Relationalism: The phenomenal character of a sensory state is constituted by the objects it makes one directly aware of.

Dispositionalism: Each color is a disposition to cause sensory states with a certain phenomenal character in normal observers in normal conditions.

Structuralism: Mathematical objects are positions in structures – e.g. the number 3 is the fourth position in the natural number structure.

I might be able to tell by introspection whether it looks to me as if there is a computer in front of me, without being able to tell by introspection whether Relationalism is true. The first is about a mental state's introspectable features. The second is about its underlying nature. I might be able to tell by perception whether a tomato is red, without being able to tell by perception whether Dispositionalism is true. The first is about the instantiation of a perceptible feature. The second is about its underlying nature. I might be able to tell by intuition whether 3 is prime, without being able to tell by intuition whether Structuralism is true. The first is about an intuitable abstract state of affairs. The second is about its underlying nature.

Even after introspecting, perceiving, and intuiting philosophers disagree about Relationalism, Dispositionalism, and Structuralism. Why? The central explanatory fact, it seems to me, is that introspection, perception, and intuition alone do not settle these claims. Premises supported by introspection, perception, and intuition can be used in philosophical arguments for or against Relationalism, Dispositionalism, and Structuralism. But the extra philosophical argumentation is required. In general these three basic sources of knowledge tell us about the "observable" aspects of their domains of application, but remain silent on the underlying natures of the items in those domains. To figure out the underlying natures of sensory phenomenology, color, and mathematical objects one needs to take into account various theoretical considerations that go beyond what introspection, perception, or intuition alone support.

The natural continuation of the pattern is this: Extreme Optimism is false; introspection can support premises that might be appealed to in philosophical arguments for or against Irreducibility; but introspection alone cannot tell us whether Irreducibility is true or false.

This is a middle ground position. Another possibility, however, is to shift to the other extreme – Extreme Pessimism. A traditional view about introspection, especially associated with Descartes, is that while one might raise skeptical challenges to our perceptual judgments about how the world outside of our experience is, our introspective judgments about how the world appears to us in our experience are secure and immune to such challenges. In opposition to this view, Eric Schwitzgebel writes:

> The introspection of current conscious experience, far from being secure, nearly infallible, is faulty, untrustworthy, and misleading – not just *possibly* mistaken, but massively and pervasively.[5]

Schwitzgebel argues for this view by citing a number of disagreements about "current conscious experience." One of those disagreements is the disagreement between proponents and opponents of cognitive phenomenology. If introspection is as unreliable as Schwitzgebel suggests, then perhaps Extreme Pessimism is warranted.

Let us focus on Irreducibility and make explicit how one might argue from disagreement to Extreme Pessimism. There are two pieces of reasoning to be considered. The first is for the claim that introspection is unreliable with respect to Irreducibility. The second is for Extreme Pessimism. Here is how we might put the first:

(1)   There are persistent disagreements among mentally similar, terminologically calibrated, unbiased, and equally introspectively reliable philosophers about Irreducibility.

(2)   If such proponents and opponents of Irreducibility persistently disagree, then it is because the proponents introspect that Irreducibility is true and the opponents introspect that Irreducibility is false.

(3)   Therefore, the capacity for introspection is unreliable with respect to Irreducibility.

Premise (1) in the argument rules out explanations of the disagreements in terms of individual differences, terminological variations, or the influence of background belief and expectation. It also rules out explanations in terms of a difference in capacities for introspection. Let us assume premise (1) is true. The conclusion (3) plausibly follows from (1) and (2). So if there is any problem with the argument is must be with (2).

And indeed there is reason to suspect (2). As noted above, introspection alone might be silent about Irreducibility. This is the idea that the disagreements about Irreducibility are due to operational constraints: just as perception does not tell you what is inside opaque containers, introspection does not tell you whether Irreducibility is true. Suppose we add such operational constraints as a possibility. Then we should revise (3) to:

(3*)   Therefore, the capacity for introspection is unreliable with respect to or silent about Irreducibility.

Now one might think that there is still a continuation of the argument that results in Extreme Pessimism. This is the second piece of reasoning:

(4)   A capacity that is unreliable with respect to or silent about Irreducibility cannot make any difference to our position to know whether Irreducibility is true.

(5)   So introspection cannot make any difference to our position to know whether Irreducibility is true – i.e. Extreme Pessimism is true.

The idea is this. If introspection is unreliable with respect to Irreducibility, then we should not rely on it in determining whether Irreducibility is true. If introspection is silent about Irreducibility, then we cannot rely on it in determining whether Irreducibility is true. Either way introspection will not help us in determining whether Irreducibility is true.

Premise (4) is false. A capacity that is unreliable with respect to or silent about Irreducibility cannot settle on its own whether Irreducibility is true. But this is different from making any difference to our position to know whether Irreducibility is true. Even if it is unreliable with respect to or silent about Irreducibility, introspection can make a difference to our position to know whether Irreducibility is true by putting us in a position to know *other facts* about our mental states that can be appealed to in philosophical arguments for or against Irreducibility.

In order to rule out this possibility the argument from disagreement would have to be strengthened so that it is about all claims about mental states that could figure in arguments for or against Irreducibility. Premise (1), for example, would have to be revised to read: there are persistent disagreements among mentally similar, terminologically calibrated, unbiased, and equally introspectively reliable philosophers about *all claims about mental states that could figure in arguments for or against Irreducibility*. Replacing "Irreducibility" with "all claims about mental states that could figure in arguments for or against Irreducibility" throughout would yield an argument that establishes Extreme Pessimism.

But there is no reason to think such an argument is sound. Philosophers disagree about Irreducibility. But they tend to agree about claims such as the following:

- I can immediately tell whether I am consciously thinking that 3 is prime.
- There is a felt difference between hearing "Dogs dogs dog dog dogs" as a mere list and hearing it as a meaningful sentence.
- There is a felt difference between merely entertaining the thought that if $a < 1$, then $2 - 2a > 0$ and intuiting that If $a < 1$, then $2 - 2a > 0$.
- Achievements such as grasping what "Dogs dogs dog dog dogs" says and intuiting that if $a < 1$, then $2 - 2a > 0$ contribute to making life interesting.

There is no reason to think there are persistent disagreements among mentally similar, terminologically calibrated, unbiased, and equally introspectively reliable philosophers about these claims. But, as we will see, these claims can figure in arguments for or against Irreducibility.

So neither Extreme Optimism nor Extreme Pessimism is warranted. Some middle ground position is the most plausible one to adopt. That said, it is difficult to give a sharp formulation to such a position. One wants to know: which of the reliable introspective judgments will be useful in philosophical arguments for or against Irreducibility? It is not clear how we might answer this question before considering particular philosophical arguments. I suggest we take an experimental approach. Let us try out different arguments that make different uses of introspective evidence and see where they get us. We begin in the next section with what initially appears to be a very indirect appeal to introspection.

The argument from introspectability

Introspection alone cannot tell you whether Irreducibility is true. In general, however, introspection alone can tell you whether you are consciously thinking that 3 is prime. One strategy that some proponents of cognitive phenomenology have pursued is to take this fact – that conscious thoughts are introspectable – as a premise in a larger philosophical argument for Irreducibility or other such theses. David Pitt has developed this sort of argument in the greatest detail.[6] In this section and the next we will focus on his work and some responses to it that opponents of cognitive phenomenology have made.

Pitt argues for a thesis he formulates as follows:

> (P) Each type of conscious thought – each state of consciously thinking that *p*, for all thinkable contents *p* – has a proprietary, distinctive, individuative phenomenology.[7]

To understand the thesis we need to see what Pitt means by "proprietary," "distinctive," and "individuative." Here is what he writes:

> I shall argue that what it is like consciously to think a particular thought is (1) different from what it is like to be in any other sort of conscious mental state (i.e., *proprietary*) and (2) different from what it is like consciously to think any other thought (i.e., *distinctive*) ... I shall also argue in this section that (3) the phenomenology of a thought *constitutes* its *representational* content (i.e., is *individuative*).[8]

Given these explanations, Pitt's thesis (P) turns out to be very strong. (P) implies both Irreducibility and Cognitive Phenomenal Intentionality, but the conjunction of Irreducibility and Cognitive Phenomenal Intentionality does not imply (P).

To see that (P) implies both Irreducibility and Cognitive Phenomenal Intentionality, consider some conscious thought that p and suppose that its phenomenology is proprietary and individuative. If its phenomenology is proprietary, then what it is like to consciously think that p is different from what it is like to be in any other sort of conscious mental state. So no wholly sensory states will suffice to put you in the same phenomenal states the conscious thought that p puts you in. Hence Irreducibility. If its phenomenology is individuative, then the phenomenology of the conscious thought that p constitutes its representational content. So the phenomenal states the conscious thought that p puts you in will suffice to put you in cognitive intentional states – specifically ones with the same representational content of the thought that p. Hence Cognitive Phenomenal Intentionality.

To see that Irreducibility and Cognitive Phenomenal Intentionality do not jointly imply (P), consider some conscious thought that p and suppose Irreducibility is true with respect to it and Cognitive Phenomenal Intentionality is true with respect to the phenomenal states it puts you in. Irreducibility implies that no wholly sensory states suffice to put you in the same phenomenal states that the conscious thought that p puts you in, but it does not imply that no cognitive states other than the thought that p suffice to put you in the same phenomenal states that the conscious thought that p puts you in. So it does not imply what Pitt calls distinctiveness, which is the second component of (P). Cognitive Phenomenal Intentionality implies that the phenomenal states the conscious thought that p puts you in will put you in some cognitive intentional state, but it does not imply that these phenomenal states will suffice to put you in cognitive intentional states with the same representational content of the thought that p. So, though similar, it is not as strong as what Pitt calls being individuative, which is the third component in (P).

Irreducibility and Cognitive Phenomenal Intentionality are controversial. So any argument that establishes a thesis that is even stronger than them is significant indeed. Let us now examine Pitt's argument.

Here is his initial formulation:

> Normally – that is, barring confusion, inattention, impaired functioning, and the like – one is able, consciously, introspectively and non-inferentially (henceforth, "Immediately") to do three distinct (but closely related) things: (a) to distinguish one's occurrent conscious thoughts from one's

other occurrent conscious mental states; (b) to distinguish one's occurrent conscious thoughts each from the others; and (c) to identify each of one's occurrent conscious thoughts as the thought it is (i.e., as having the *content* it does). But (the argument continues), one would not be able to do these things unless each (type of) occurrent conscious thought had a phenomenology that is (1) different from that of any other type of conscious mental state (proprietary), (2) different from that of any other type of conscious thought (distinct), and (3) constitutive of its (representational) content (individuative) ... Hence (the argument concludes), each type of conscious thought has a proprietary, unique phenomenology, which constitutes its representational content.[9]

The basic form of Pitt's argument might be rendered as follows: we can Φ; we couldn't Φ unless p; therefore, p. We can immediately distinguish and identify our conscious thoughts; we couldn't distinguish and identify our conscious thoughts unless (P); therefore, (P). This form of argument is valid. So if there is a problem with it the problem is with one of the premises.

The premises deploy two notions that require explication. These are: distinguishing a mental state (in particular a conscious thought) from other mental states, and identifying a mental state (in particular a conscious thought) as the mental state it is. Pitt explains these notions by reference to two notions from Dretske's early work on perception and perceptual knowledge.

The first is what Dretske calls "non-epistemic seeing." Here is how Dretske explains this notion:

S sees$_n$ D = D is visually differentiated from its immediate environment by S.[10]

By "visually differentiated" Dretske means that "S's differentiation of D is constituted by D's *looking some way* to S and, moreover, looking different than its immediate environment."[11] Note the similarity to how I explained the notion of awareness in the introduction. There I said that states of awareness enable demonstrative thoughts about objects of awareness at least in part because they phenomenally differentiate objects of awareness (pp. 12–13). Awareness so characterized is a determinable relation. One determination of it is visual awareness, in which objects of awareness are phenomenally differentiated by how they look. Plausibly, then, Dretske's notion of non-epistemic seeing should be identified with visual awareness.

The second notion from Dretske that Pitt appeals to is what Dretske calls "primary epistemic seeing." What makes primary epistemic seeing epistemic is that unlike non-epistemic seeing it necessarily includes the formation of a belief that amounts to knowledge. You do not form beliefs about everything you see. For example, you might see a flat-tailed horned lizard, and it might be a fine specimen of its kind, but you might not form any belief about the matter. If you do form such a belief, however, then you might do so in a way that counts as primary epistemic seeing. Dretske gives a set of necessary and sufficient conditions for when a subject S sees that an object of non-epistemic seeing b has some property P. These are:

(i) b is P
(ii) S sees$_n$ b
(iii) The conditions under which S sees$_n$ b are such that b would not look, L, the way it now looks to S unless it was P.
(iv) S, believing the conditions are as described in (iii), takes b to be P.

Notice that Dretske's analysis of primary epistemic seeing does not use the notion of knowledge. This is because he is contributing to the project of analyzing knowledge in more basic terms. But we are not trying to do that here. For our purposes the important thing is to isolate the notion of primary epistemic seeing and make sure we got the right notion in mind. If we use the notion of knowledge, then it is a simple matter to explain primary epistemic seeing. For you to see that the lizard is a fine specimen of the flat-tailed horned lizard in the primary epistemic sense is for you to know that the lizard is a fine specimen of the flat-tailed horned lizard on the basis of how the lizard looks to you when you are visually aware of it. And in general S sees that b is P in the primary epistemic sense just in case S knows that b is P on the basis of how b looks to S when S is visually aware of b.

Just as visual awareness is one form of awareness, so primary epistemic seeing is one form of knowledge based on awareness. We can explain this more general notion of knowledge based on awareness as follows: S knows that b is P on the basis of awareness just in case S knows that b is P on the basis of how b appears to S when S is aware of b. Pitt uses the terms "acquaintance" and "knowledge by acquaintance" for what I am calling awareness and knowledge based on awareness. The terms Pitt chooses, however, have a history. Bertrand Russell used them as technical terms in developing his views about experience, judgment, and language. We will discuss some of these views in chapter 6. But Pitt's argument need not depend on Russell's distinctive views about these matters. In order to keep this point clear I will substitute "awareness" and "knowledge based on awareness" for "acquaintance" and "knowledge by acquaintance."

We have illustrated awareness and knowledge based on awareness using sensory perceptual examples. But the scope of these notions extends further than sensory perception. Plausibly we are also aware of and have knowledge based on awareness of our own mental states. Pinch yourself. The feeling associated with this pinch is a conscious mental state. Its immediate environment is your other contemporaneous or near contemporaneous conscious mental states. And it is phenomenally differentiated from these: the felt pinch stands out as different from your sensory perceptual experiences and other bodily sensations. So there is no problem in saying that you are aware of the felt pinch. Further you know something about it in virtue of how it appears when you are aware of the felt pinch. For example, you know that it feels different from an itch. So there is no problem in saying that you have knowledge based on awareness of the felt pinch.

Now recall that we got into this discussion of awareness and knowledge based on awareness because we wanted to gain some insight into Pitt's notions of distinguishing and identifying a conscious thought. Given the foregoing, it is easy to do so. These notions encapsulate the idea that awareness and knowledge based on awareness extend to our own conscious thoughts. Distinguishing a conscious thought is being aware of it. Identifying a conscious thought is knowing on the basis of awareness of it what thought it is. Notice that if S knows on the basis of awareness of M that M is a thought that p, then the object of S's awareness is M itself. So identifying a conscious thought presupposes distinguishing it. It follows that ability (c) in Pitt's argument quoted above (pp. 31–2) presupposes abilities (a) and (b). Further, if S is aware of M, then M is phenomenally differentiated from S's other contemporaneous or near contemporaneous conscious mental states, whether these be other conscious thoughts or not. That is, abilities (a) and (b) in Pitt's argument come together as a package.

It is possible, then, to formulate Pitt's argument in a way that focuses on the identification of conscious thoughts. And this is what Pitt does when he summarizes things:

> In brief:
>
> (K1) It is possible Immediately to identify one's occurrent conscious thoughts (equivalently (see below): one can know by acquaintance [i.e. on

the basis of awareness] *which* thought a particular occurrent conscious thought is); but

(K2) It would not be possible Immediately to identify one's conscious thoughts unless each type of conscious thought had a proprietary, distinctive, individuative phenomenology [thus unless at least Irreducibility and Phenomenal Intentionality are both true]; so

(P) Each type of conscious thought – each state of consciously thinking that *p*, for all thinkable contents *p* – has a proprietary, distinctive, individuative phenomenology [thus Irreducibility and Phenomenal Intentionality are both true].[12]

I have made some additions in brackets that calibrate Pitt's preferred formulations with those adopted here. As noted above, the argument is valid. Now that we have explored the meaning of its premises, it will be easier to assess their plausibility.

Assessing the argument from introspectability

Joseph Levine writes:

> What it is to have knowledge of what one is thinking is to token a mental representation – a mentalese sentence – that expresses the fact that one is thinking what one is thinking. What makes this Immediate knowledge, in Pitt's sense, is the fact that this sentence tokening is not the result of an inferential process, but rather an immediate causal result of the first-order thought state itself (together with some functionally characterizable internal monitoring process). It's because of the reliability of the relevant process yielding the higher-order sentence expressing the fact that one is thinking a certain content that it counts as knowledge. If this explanation is adequate, then we don't need to appeal to the thought's phenomenal character to explain how we know – Immediately – that we're thinking it.[13]

In a similar vein Michael Tye and Briggs Wright write:

> Let us grant that introspective knowledge of what we are occurently thinking is not baseless. Rather, it is based on evidence that we can introspect. It might be suggested that the relevant evidence here consists in introspective beliefs that provide evidential reasons. Intuitively, however, our evidence for believing that we are thinking that *P* does not consist in

further beliefs at all. Intuitively, we have introspective access to certain mental states, and these states are our evidence for introspective beliefs without providing a propositional justification for those beliefs.

On this reliabilist view of introspective knowledge, introspective beliefs are warranted because of their causal ancestry, which will include the introspected mental states in question.[14]

Levine, Tye, and Wright describe ways of coming to know what one is consciously thinking that do not depend on one's conscious thought having any phenomenal character.

They share the same basic idea, which is that knowledge of what one is consciously thinking can be explained by a reliable mechanism. Suppose M is one's conscious thought that p and B is one's belief that one is consciously thinking that p. Why does B amount to knowledge? According to Pitt B amounts to knowledge because it is based on how M appears to one while one is aware of M. According to Levine and to Tye and Wright B amounts to knowledge because there is in our psychological tool kit a reliable mechanism that takes a mental state as input and returns a belief that one is in that mental state as output and B is the result of this mechanism operating on M. Their contrasting account does not depend on M having any appearance. Let's call Pitt's account the awareness-based account and the contrasting account promoted by Levine, Tye, and Wright the reliabilist account.

It is not immediately clear how the reliabilist account is supposed to challenge Pitt's argument. Which premise does it challenge? One thing Levine writes – that his reliabilist account explains "what makes this [belief about what one is consciously thinking] immediate knowledge, *in Pitt's sense*" – suggests that the answer to this question is the second premise, (K2). Pitt points out some phenomenon in the first premise. And his second premise is that the only explanation for the phenomenon is his awareness-based account. The challenge posed by Levine, Tye, and Wright, then, is that the second premise is false because there is also the reliabilist account. So Pitt's argument is at least incomplete: he needs to show that the awareness-based account is a better explanation than the reliabilist account.

This is one way to take the challenge, but I do not think it is the best way to take it, and I do not think this is how the parties to the debate in fact understand it. Rather, the challenge Levine, Tye, and Wright make is to Pitt's first premise. Instead of accepting Pitt's characterization of the phenomenon and offering an alternative explanation of it, they reject his characterization itself. And this makes sense because Pitt's characterization of the phenomenon is very loaded. He does not just make the uncontroversial observation that we often know by introspection what we are consciously thinking. Rather, he makes the controversial claim that we often know what we are consciously thinking on the basis of how our conscious thoughts appear to us when we are aware of them. That it is on the basis of awareness is built into Pitt's description of the phenomenon. His explanation in the second premise is not of why our belief amounts to knowledge; rather, it is of why the awareness-based account of why our belief amounts to knowledge works.

So the disagreement is this: according to Pitt, reflection on typical cases shows that we know what we are consciously thinking in a way that fits the awareness-based account; according to Levine, Tye, and Wright reflection on typical cases is compatible with the view that we know what we are consciously thinking in a way that fits the reliabilist account.

The problem with this result, however, is that now we run the danger of overworking introspection. In the second section ('The Role of Introspection') we considered the prospects of introspecting whether Irreducibility is true. The prospects looked dim. Irreducibility lies outside the scope of direct introspection. Pitt's argument was supposed to get beyond this problem by refocusing things on the fact that introspection tells us what we are consciously thinking. Our conscious thoughts lie inside the scope of direct introspection. But now we see that Pitt's argument depends on a premise not just to the effect *that* we can introspect our thoughts, but also on a premise about what this introspection *consists in* – a premise to the effect that when we introspect our thoughts our knowledge of them is based on how they appear when we are aware of them. And it looks as if this premise itself is supposed to be supported by introspection.

So Pitt appeals to introspection in supporting a claim about what introspection consists in. Levine, Tye, and Wright dispute the introspective support. According to them introspection might consist in a reliable process that works independently of awareness. They need not claim that introspection itself supports adopting the reliabilist account of introspection. All they need to claim is that introspection itself is neutral between the awareness-based account and the reliabilist account. In sum: introspection tells us what we are consciously thinking; and maybe introspection tells us that introspection tells us what we are consciously thinking; but – Levine, Tye, and Wright could argue – introspection does not tell us about its own underlying nature, specifically about the nature of the mechanism by which it tells us what we are consciously thinking.

The upshot is that Pitt's first premise requires more support. One might make the case that introspection really does tell us about its own workings and that these workings fit the awareness-based account. Or one might develop an argument for the awareness-based account that appeals to considerations beyond those introspection alone provides.

One possibility of this second sort is to rely on background theses in general epistemology. The most relevant issue in general epistemology is the dispute between epistemic internalists and epistemic externalists. This is a complicated issue that deserves and has received book-length treatments of its own. Here I can only indicate how it bears on the dispute between Pitt and his critics.

According to epistemic internalists facts about what one is justified in believing are determined by facts one is in a position to know about by reflection alone – i.e. by introspection and a priori reasoning. These include facts about one's own conscious mental states and logical relations. But they exclude facts about the reliability of one's psychological mechanisms. According to epistemic externalists facts about what one is justified in believing can also depend on facts one might not be in a position to know about by reflection alone. These include facts about the reliability of one's psychological mechanisms.

The reliabilist account that Levine, Tye, and Wright defend is an epistemic externalist account of introspection. Suppose it is the best externalist account: if you are an externalist, it is the one you should adopt. The awareness-based account that Pitt defends is an epistemic internalist account of introspection. Suppose it is the best internalist account: if you are an internalist, it is the one you should adopt. Then one might develop an internalist argument for Pitt's awareness-based account as follows. First, epistemic internalism is preferable to epistemic externalism. Second, the awareness-based account is preferable to any other internalist account of introspection of conscious thoughts. Therefore Pitt's awareness-based account is preferable to all others and is the one we should adopt.

This is not intended to be an actual argument for the awareness-based account. Rather it is an indication of one line a proponent of the awareness-based account might pursue. If it proves workable, then there is reason to accept Pitt's first premise, (K1).

Now let us consider challenges to Pitt's second premise. Tye and Wright mount one:

Consider a case of simple seeing – my seeing a ripe tomato, say. In seeing a tomato, I am conscious of it. It looks red and round to me. What has phenomenal character here is not the tomato – the thing of which I am conscious – but my consciousness of it. Generally, for M to be experienced some way by S is not a matter of M's phenomenology but rather of M causing in S a state with some phenomenology or other. Correspondingly, if introspective awareness of a particular thought, t, is like seeing a tomato, what has phenomenal character is not t but my introspective consciousness of t.[15]

The point about perception is correct. If I know that a tomato is red by how it looks to me when I see it, what has a phenomenal character is my visual experience, not the tomato. Tye and Wright suggest that if Pitt consistently applies the awareness-based account to knowledge of conscious thoughts, then a parallel claim should hold. That is: if I know that I am consciously thinking that p by how it appears to me when I am aware of my thought that p, what has phenomenal character is my introspective experience, not the thought that p.

There are at least two replies one might make on behalf of Pitt.

One concedes the point to Tye and Wright, but notes that Tye and Wright's point does not clearly undermine Pitt's premise (K2). If the awareness-based account applies, then conscious thoughts have appearances, and it isn't clear what these appearances can be other than phenomenal characters, even if they are different phenomenal characters from those possessed by introspective experiences of conscious thoughts. Whether these phenomenal characters must also be proprietary, distinctive, and individuative is another question – to which we will return below.

The second reply aims to identify appearances of conscious thoughts with phenomenal characters possessed by introspective experiences of conscious thoughts. If the object of awareness and the awareness are the same, then if the awareness has a phenomenal character so does the object of awareness. In the case of perceptual awareness the identity is implausible. A tomato is one thing; your perceptual awareness of the tomato is another thing. So the tomato need not have the phenomenal character of your awareness of the tomato. In the case of awareness of conscious thoughts, however, perhaps the identity is defensible. Conscious thoughts are experiences. Maybe, then, they are in part experiences of themselves. On this view, a conscious thought is one thing; your introspective awareness of the conscious thought is the very same thing. So the conscious thought must have the same phenomenal character as your awareness of the conscious thought.

Consider the following from Horgan, Tienson, and Graham:

> Sensory-phenomenal states do not merely present apparent objects and properties to the experiencer – for instance, redness, as an apparent property of an apparent object in one's visual field. In addition, they present *themselves*, since a given phenomenal state-type *is* a specific type of phenomenal character. There is something that *experiencing* red is like. Visual experience of red objects acquaints you not merely with those objects and *their* redness, but with the distinctive what-it's-like-to-experience-redness character of the experience itself.[16]

Call the sort of awareness Horgan *et al.* are describing self-presentational awareness.[17] Two clarifications about it are in order.

First, it is not restricted to sensory states. As Horgan *et al.* make clear, the motivation for postulating self-presentational awareness is phenomenal consciousness as such, not anything special about sensory phenomenal consciousness. One might worry that taking conscious thoughts to be self-presentational is question begging. But it is not. That conscious thoughts are phenomenally conscious is not in question. What is in question is whether their phenomenal characters have the additional features Pitt claims for them.

Second, self-presentational awareness is not the same as introspective knowledge. Self-presentational awareness is pre-reflective: it automatically comes along with all phenomenally conscious states, and it typically occurs without giving rise to associated beliefs. Introspective knowledge, however, is reflective: it is directed by our intention to gain knowledge about ourselves, and it typically gives rise to associated beliefs.[18] Self-presentational awareness is a form of awareness, and analogous to seeing, not a form of self-knowledge, which would be analogous to perceptual knowledge based on seeing.

If awareness of conscious thoughts is self-presentational awareness, then Tye and Wright are mistaken about the implications of applying the awareness-based account for knowledge of conscious thoughts. So far, then, Pitt's premise (K2) looks to be in pretty good shape.

There is, however, another way to challenge Pitt's second premise. It is similar to Tye and Wright's challenge in that it derives from reflection on how the awareness-based account works in the case of perception.

Suppose you know that a tomato is red by how it looks to you when you see it. Notice that this is compatible with two facts. First, something that is not a red tomato could appear exactly the same way as the red tomato appears to you. It could be a hologram or another kind of fruit with a different color that is positioned and lit just so that it looks the way a red tomato should. The possibilities are endless. Second, something that is a red tomato could appear to you to be other than a red tomato. This could be due to weird environmental effects or some atypical condition you are in. Again, the possibilities are endless. So, even though you know that the tomato is red by how it looks to you when you see it, it does not follow that (i) nothing other than a tomato could look that way, (ii) nothing other than a red tomato could look that way, or (iii) such a look implies the presence of a red tomato. That is: the looks of red tomatoes need not be proprietary, distinctive, or individuative in order for one to know that a tomato is red by how it looks. So why should the appearance of a conscious thought that p have to be proprietary, distinctive, and indviduative in order for one to know that a conscious thought is a thought that p by how it appears?

So this worry concedes two things to Pitt: it concedes that we often know about our conscious thoughts by being aware of them, and it concedes that they have phenomenal characters. The worry challenges Pitt's view of the nature of this phenomenal character: it questions whether it must be proprietary, distinctive, and individuative. If the phenomenal character need not have these features, then perhaps the phenomenal states that enable knowledge of our conscious thoughts on the basis of awareness are reducible to wholly sensory phenomenal states.

I'm inclined to think this is a serious worry for Pitt's argument. If the looks of tomatoes were proprietary, distinctive, and individuative then perceptual beliefs based on the looks of tomatoes would be infallible. That is, you couldn't mistakenly come to believe that a tomato is red on the basis of how it looks to you. If it looked that way to you, then it would have to be red. But there is no reason to think perceptual beliefs based on the looks of tomatoes are infallible. You might very well mistakenly come to believe that a tomato is red on the basis of how it looks to you. So there is no reason to think the looks of tomatoes are proprietary, distinctive, and individuative.

What about introspection? Introspection in general is fallible. It is not immediately clear why introspection of our own conscious thoughts would be special. Surely it often gets things right. But why think that it must, that it is impossible for you to mistakenly come to believe you are having a thought of a certain kind on the basis of how it appears to you? Some philosophers have argued that such mistakes occur when we think we are entertaining a demonstrative thought about something but there is no thing we could genuinely demonstrate.[19] For example, when Macbeth says to himself, "Is this a dagger which I see before me, the handle toward my hand?" then he might also believe of himself, I am entertaining a demonstrative thought about a dagger, and this belief might be formed on the basis of how the thought he gives expression to in his soliloquy appears to him. But, at least on some views, his belief about his own thought would be mistaken since there is no dagger for him to genuinely demonstrate.

Suppose mistakes along these lines are possible. Then even if the awareness-based account is correct and our knowledge of our own conscious thoughts is based on how they appear, it need not be that their appearances are proprietary, distinctive, and individuative. One aggressive response to this line of argument is to reject the possibility that we can form mistaken beliefs about our own conscious thoughts on the basis of awareness of them. One concessive response is to admit that mistakes are possible in some cases but argue that there are special cases in which it is not possible and that these special cases are sufficient to make Pitt's argument work. Neither response is closed off by any of the foregoing. Perhaps one is workable, but it is not obvious either way. So Pitt's argument at least requires further supplementation.

Summary

The results of this chapter are largely negative. Introspection alone will not settle the various disputes about cognitive phenomenology. And arguments based on the introspectability of conscious thoughts turn out to be inconclusive. One positive result, however, is that we need not forego introspection altogether. Introspection can supply premises to other possible philosophical arguments for or against Irreducibility. In the next few chapters we will consider a number of such arguments.

Notes

1 Siewert 1998, 276–277.
2 Tye and Wright 2011, 329–330.
3 Bayne and Spener 2010.
4 See Siewert 2011 for a careful attempt to explain "phenomenal state," "what it is like," "phenomenal character," and related terms in a way that

does not assign them a meaning that restricts their application to states phenomenally similar to itches, bodily sensations, visual perceptions, and the like.

5 Schwitzgebel 2008, 259.

6 See also Goldman 1993.

7 Pitt 2004, 5.

8 Ibid., 3–4.

9 Ibid., 7–8.

10 Dretske 1969, 20. "Sees$_n$" is Dretske's shorthand for non-epistemic seeing.

11 Ibid., 20.

12 Pitt 2004, 8.

13 Levine 2011, 106–107.

14 Tye and Wright 2011, 340.

15 Ibid., 339.

16 Horgan *et al.* 2006, 54.

17 Kriegel and Williford 2006 provide a good entry way into the literature on this notion.

18 See Zahavi 2005 and Gallagher and Zahavi 2012 for further discussion of the pre-reflective/reflective distinction.

19 See Evans 1982 and McDowell 1986.

Further reading

Schwitzgebel (2008) and Bayne and Spener (2010) are good places to start exploring the reliability of introspection. Spener (2011) specifically discusses introspection in the context of debates about cognitive phenomenology. David Pitt develops his argument from introspectability in Pitt (2004, 2011). See Levine (2011) and Tye and Wright (2011) for criticisms of Pitt's argument.

2

CONTRAST

In the previous chapter we considered some introspective judgments that philosophers tend to agree on. Two of these were:

- There is a felt difference between hearing "Dogs dogs dog dog dogs" as a mere list and hearing it as a meaningful sentence.
- There is a felt difference between merely entertaining the thought that if $a < 1$, then $2 - 2a > 0$ and intuiting that if $a < 1$, then $2 - 2a > 0$.

In this chapter we will explore attempts to work claims like these into arguments for Irreducibility. The arguments we will consider are called phenomenal contrast arguments. Their ambition is to take uncontroversial, introspectively known claims about phenomenal differences as premises in arguments that support controversial claims such as Irreducibility.

I distinguish three sorts of phenomenal contrast argument. All rely on premises about the phenomenal characters of some mental states. Arguments of the first sort rely solely on premises about the phenomenal differences between mental states. I will call these pure phenomenal contrast arguments. In my view these arguments are not that strong. Arguments of the second and third sort represent different ways of strengthening the phenomenal contrast approach to establishing Irreducibility. Arguments of the second sort rely on premises about phenomenal differences between the mental states of hypothetical people that lack all sensory phenomenology. I will call these hypothetical phenomenal contrast arguments. In my view these arguments are problematic. Arguments of the third sort do not rely solely on premises about the phenomenal differences between mental states. They also rely on premises that provide a gloss on these phenomenal differences. I will call these glossed phenomenal contrast arguments. In my view there is a sound glossed phenomenal contrast argument for Irreducibility.

Each of the sections below deals with one of the three sorts of phenomenal contrast argument.

Pure phenomenal contrast arguments

Let's say that a case is an actual or possible scenario in which a subject is in some phenomenal states. A phenomenal contrast consists of a pair of cases that differ with respect to what phenomenal states their subjects are in.

One reason phenomenal contrasts are useful is that they help draw attention to certain phenomenal states. This was the use I made of them in the introduction, with the examples of seeing, emotionally reacting, intuiting, and understanding. We might call this the ostensive use of phenomenal contrasts. By a phenomenal contrast argument I have something else in mind.[1] The aim of a phenomenal contrast argument is not merely to point to some phenomenal states, but to establish some thesis about the nature of those states. By a pure phenomenal contrast argument I mean an argument that purports to establish such a thesis by reasoning about the mere existence of a phenomenal contrast. These arguments typically take the form of inferences to the best explanation.

Here is a well-known example from the literature:

> Philosophers will ask whether there is really such a thing as understanding-experience, over and above visual experience, auditory experience, and so on ... This question may be asked: does the difference between Jacques (a monoglot Frenchman) and Jack (a monoglot Englishman), as they listen to the news in French, really consist in the Frenchman's having a different *experience*? ... The present claim is simply that Jacques's experience when listening to the news is utterly different from Jack's, and that this is so even though there is a sense in which Jacques and Jack have the same aural experience.
>
> It is certainly true that Jacques's experience when listening to the news is very different from Jack's. And the difference between the two can be

expressed by saying that Jacques, when exposed to the stream of sound, has what one may perfectly well call "an experience (as) of understanding" or "an understanding-experience," while Jack does not.[2]

The phenomenal contrast consists of the following pair of cases:

Jacques's Case: Hearing the news with understanding.

Jack's Case: Hearing the news without understanding.

Here is one way we might put the inference to the best explanation:

(1) Jacques's Case and Jack's Case contain different phenomenal states.
(2) Jacques's Case and Jack's Case contain the same sensory states.
(3) Jacques's Case and Jack's Case contain different cognitive states.
(4) The only candidate explanations for the difference in the phenomenal states are a difference in the sensory states or a difference in the cognitive states.
(5) The best explanation for the difference in the phenomenal states is the difference in the cognitive states.
(6) So there are some phenomenal states such that cognitive states and not sensory states put one in them.

This particular phenomenal contrast argument is problematic in three ways. First, premise (2) is dubious. Second, premise (3) is at least questionable. Third, the conclusion (6) falls short of Irreducibility. I will discuss each of these problems below. Considering different cases or making the reasoning more nuanced can repair some. But others remain.

I will assume that premises (1) and (4) are OK. Premise (1) comes from the phenomenal contrast, and seems unassailable. Premise (4) can be dispensed with for more nuanced claims, but is a useful and unproblematic simplification in the present context. Claim (5) follows from (1) through (4).

Let us start with premise (2). A number of philosophers have argued that it is false, that the two cases contain different sensory states.[3] For example, Jacques might hear the stream of sounds as structured into words and sentences and he might have visual imagery corresponding to various topics discussed in the news. In response, one might argue that these differences, even if they exist, are not capable of explaining all the phenomenal differences between the two cases. It is worth noting that (2) is stronger than the claim Strawson makes. Strawson says that, "there is a sense in which Jacques and Jack have the same aural experience." This leaves open that there is a sense in which their aural experiences are different, and it also leaves open the possibility of other sensory differences. Strawson's idea, then, must be that it is not necessary to rule out the possibility of any sensory differences. All the inference to the best explanation requires is that whatever sensory differences there might be are not of the right sort to explain all the phenomenal differences between the two cases. This is surely correct, but it is difficult to see how to adjudicate the debate between someone who thinks there are explanatorily sufficient sensory differences and someone who thinks that whatever sensory differences there might be are explanatorily insufficient. Without some way of settling this issue the pure phenomenal contrast argument does not do much to help the case for irreducible cognitive phenomenology.

Considering an expanded range of phenomenal contrast might suggest that for at least some contrasts there are phenomenal differences in the absence of explanatorily sufficient sensory differences. The literature now contains many examples to choose from. As mentioned above, there is the felt difference between hearing "Dogs dogs dog dog dogs" as a mere list and hearing it as a meaningful sentence. There is the felt difference between hearing "Let's meet at the bank" as suggesting a rendezvous by a financial institution and as suggesting a rendezvous by a body of water. One of my favorite phenomenal contrasts is that which occurs between reading the following passage before knowing its key word and reading it after knowing its key word:

> A newspaper is better than a magazine. A seashore is a better place than the street. At first it is better to run than to walk. You may have to try several times. It takes some skill but it is easy to learn. Even young children can enjoy it. Once successful, complications are minimal. Birds seldom get too close. Rain, however, soaks in very fast. Too many people doing the same thing can also cause problems. One needs lots of room. If there are no complications it can be very peaceful. A rock will serve as an anchor. If things break loose from it, however, you will not get a second chance.[4]

The key word is "kite." Here we have a felt difference between reading a passage without getting its meaning and reading a passage while getting its meaning. The list can be extended.[5] It is not clear to me, however, that considering more cases adds to the dialectical power of pure phenomenal contrast arguments. Someone persuaded that there is irreducible cognitive phenomenology will find further illustrations of it. Someone skeptical about irreducible cognitive phenomenology will think that careful inspection will always turn up some explanatorily sufficient sensory differences.

Let us turn to premise (3). It is questionable because there are competing views about the nature of the relevant form of linguistic understanding. One view is that it is an at least partly cognitive mental state. On this view premise (3) is true. Another view is that it is a wholly sensory mental state. On this view premise (3) is false. The view that the understanding is a wholly sensory mental state depends on the idea that sensory mental states might have high-level content. I mentioned this idea in the introduction. Low-level contents represent properties such as shapes, colors, sounds, smells, etc. High-level contents represent properties such as meanings, natural kinds, artifactual kinds, and causal relations. Someone who thinks that the understanding is a wholly sensory state, then, will think that it is a wholly sensory state with high-level content attributing semantic properties to some perceived interpretable item such as an inscription or an utterance.[6]

Two clarifications about this view are in order. First, the view is not that the relevant form of understanding is partly sensory and partly cognitive: it is not that there is a sensory part representing shapes or sounds and a cognitive part representing semantic properties. There is no part of the understanding that is free from awareness of or seeming awareness of environmental witnesses to the instantiation of the semantic properties it represents. Second, the view does not imply that when you understand something you are or seem to be aware of spooky entities – meanings floating around in your spatiotemporal vicinity. The environmental witnesses to the instantiation of semantic properties might just be ordinary low-level audible and visible features of speech and writing. If understanding is a wholly sensory state it does not follow that meanings are objects of auditory or visual awareness. All that follows is that states of understanding represent semantic properties in ways that depend on awareness or seeming awareness of indicators – which might be looks and sounds – of their instantiation.

It is not clear to me which view – the partly cognitive view or the wholly sensory view – of the understanding is correct. It would be rash to make an assessment without taking into account empirical work on semantic perception.[7] This need not stall the attempt to support Irreducibility by a pure phenomenal contrast argument however. Recall Siewert's example of shifts in thought quoted at the beginning of the previous chapter.[8] There is a felt difference between engaging in an activity (reading, watching TV, whatever) without interruption and having that activity interrupted by a sudden thought, e.g. a recollection of an appointment. In such cases there is no attribution of semantic properties to a perceived interpretable item. So it doesn't matter whether such attributions – states of understanding – are wholly sensory. The phenomenal contrasts involved in shifts in thought clearly include changes in cognitive mental states. So the sort of worries attaching to premise (3) would not come up for a pure phenomenal contrast argument constructed around them. Still, there are the worries attaching to premise (2). Shifts in thought are typically accompanied by sensory differences, and opponents of cognitive phenomenology would argue that it is those that account for the phenomenal differences.

Finally let us consider the conclusion of the argument, (6). This says: there are some phenomenal states such that cognitive states and not sensory states put one in them. But Irreducibility says something else: some cognitive states put one in phenomenal states for which no wholly sensory states suffice. There is a gap between the two claims. To see it, we need to take into account the fact that many states are partly cognitive and partly sensory. The state of understanding the news, for example, includes hearing the news. So the significance of (6) is: there are some phenomenal states such that partly cognitive states and not wholly sensory states put one in them. Suppose this is true: there is some case in which a partly cognitive state but not a wholly sensory state puts you in some phenomenal state. It does not follow that there are no wholly sensory states that could have put you in the same phenomenal state. Maybe a partly cognitive state puts you in some phenomenal state, but maybe the phenomenal state it puts you in is no different in kind from the sort of phenomenal state a wholly sensory state might have put you in. Even if that wholly sensory state does not occur on the occasion in question, it still might be a sufficient condition when it does occur for the relevant phenomenal state.

Given these three difficulties, proponents of cognitive phenomenology should look for more solid ground on which to support their view than is provided by pure phenomenal contrast arguments.

Hypothetical phenomenal contrast arguments

A natural way to address the challenges to pure phenomenal contrast arguments is to construct a phenomenal contrast argument on the basis of a pair of cases in which it is guaranteed that there is no change in sensory state whatsoever. Such pairs of cases do not actually occur. But perhaps they could. Hence the name "hypothetical phenomenal contrast argument."

In recent work Uriah Kriegel has developed an argument that can be construed as a hypothetical phenomenal contrast argument.[9] Kriegel argues for a thesis stronger than Irreducibility. He argues for the thesis I called Independence, which says: some cognitive states put one in phenomenal states that are independent of sensory states. Since Independence implies Irreducibility, any argument that establishes Independence establishes Irreducibility.

Acceptance of Independence is equivalent to belief in purely cognitive phenomenal states. These are phenomenal states for which wholly cognitive states suffice. Kriegel argues for Independence by getting us to imagine a person – Zoe – whose total phenomenal state is supposed to include cognitive phenomenal states but not include any sensory phenomenal states. It is made up of purely cognitive phenomenal states. Kriegel brings Zoe to imaginative life in three stages.

The first stage is to imagine some partial zombies. Whereas complete zombies are creatures that have internal states that function just like the mental states of normal humans but without having any phenomenal states, partial zombies are creatures that have internal states that function just like the mental states of normal humans but without having any phenomenal states of certain kinds.[10] A visual zombie, for example, would have internal states that function just like the mental states associated with normal human vision and visualization but would not have any visual phenomenal states. This is the sort of partial zombie Kriegel starts with: "imagine a person whose visual cortex is so dysfunctional that it produces no visual states. This person is congenitally blind, but – let us suppose – she is also more than that: she is incapable not only of *vision* but also of *visualization*. She is, in Horgan's phrase, a *partial zombie* – specifically, a *visual zombie*."[11] It is a short step to imagining a complete sensory zombie, where "sensory" here means pertaining to the five senses. So this person lacks visual, auditory, tactile, gustatory, and olfactory phenomenal states. Next imagine an algedonic zombie – someone who cannot feel pleasure or pain. Finally imagine an emotional zombie. Each of these partial zombies seems individually imaginable.

The second stage in Kriegel's portrait of Zoe is to put all the partial zombies together: "perform another act of imaginative synthesis and envisage a person lacking all of these phenomenologies [sensory, algedonic, emotional] at once."[12] The idea is that just as you might imagine a sensory zombie by synthesizing visual, auditory, tactile, gustatory, and olfactory zombies, so you might imagine a sensory-algedonic-emotional zombie by synthesizing a sensory zombie, an algedonic zombie, and an emotional zombie.

The third and final stage is to make a stipulation about the person imagined in the second stage: "she happens to be a mathematical genius, and spends her days effectively (re)developing elementary geometry and arithmetic. In her darkened world of sensory, algedonic, and emotional emptiness, she avoids boredom by formulating mathematical propositions, thinking informally about their plausibility, and then trying to prove them from axioms she has provisionally set."[13]

In order to support Independence Kriegel needs to make a further claim about the results of our imaginative endeavors, namely that Zoe has phenomenal states. He does so by arguing that there is a phenomenal contrast. In particular, he considers cases in which Zoe suddenly realizes how a proof ought to go. For example, suppose Zoe conjectures that there are an infinite number of prime numbers. She knows that if there is only a finite number of prime numbers then there is a list of them from first to last $p_1, p_2, p_3, \ldots p_n$. But how can she use this fact in a proof? ... Suddenly she sees how: Let $P = p_1, p_2, p_3, \ldots p_n + 1$. P is prime or not. If P is prime, then P is a prime not on the list. If P is not prime, then P is divisible by some prime not on the list since division by any of those leaves a remainder of 1. So there must be an infinite number of prime numbers.

According to Kriegel there is a phenomenal contrast between the case in which Zoe fails to have the sudden realization and the case in which Zoe succeeds in having the sudden realization. This is like Siewert's shift-in-thought example. But it is supposed to occur in the absence of any sensory phenomenology, since Zoe is a sensory-algedonic-emotional zombie. That is what makes it a hypothetical rather than a pure phenomenal contrast. One additional twist in Kriegel's discussion is that he does not just assume that the contrast associated with Zoe's realization is phenomenal. He gives an argument for this claim. I return to the argument below. If Kriegel's claim that there is a phenomenal contrast is true, then Zoe's total phenomenal state at the time of the realization is an example of a total phenomenal state that includes cognitive phenomenal states but does not include any sensory phenomenal states. And so there are purely cognitive phenomenal states – those that make up Zoe's total phenomenal state at the time of the realization – and Independence and Irreducibility are both true.

One weakness in Kriegel's argument is that an opponent of cognitive phenomenology might concede that Zoe is imaginable in some sense, but not the right sense for establishing her possibility. Kriegel says he can conceive of Zoe, and so a situation in which there are total phenomenal states that include cognitive phenomenal states but not sensory phenomenal states. Adam Pautz demurs. Here is what he writes about hypothetical cases of the sort Kriegel describes:

> we *cannot* positively imagine such a case. At least *I* cannot. Just try. If [there is a possible case of cognitive phenomenal states without sensory phenomenal states], then in such a case we have a rich phenomenal life that *overlaps* with our actual phenomenal life, only it is totally non-sensory. But what would it be like? Can you imagine this overlapping phenomenology? If you try to imagine what it would be like, you might imagine seeing all black, having an experience of inner speech ("nothing much is happening"), and so on. But then you will not be imagining a case in which you have cognitive phenomenal properties but *no* sensory properties.[14]

This passage occurs in the context of an argument against Irreducibility. I will explore that argument in chapter 5. For present purposes the key point is that Pautz denies being about to "positively imagine" precisely what Kriegel claims to be conceivable.

One explanation of their different claims is that there is a relevant gap between conceiving and positively imagining. The background here is work on modal epistemology, especially that of Yablo and Chalmers. Chalmers distinguishes between positive and negative conceivability:

> The central sort of negative conceivability holds that S is negatively conceivable when S is not ruled out a priori, or when there is no (apparent) contradiction in S. ...
>
> Positive notions of conceivability require that one can form some sort of positive conception of a situation in which S is the case. One can place the varieties of positive conceivability under the broad rubric of *imagination*: to positively conceive of a situation is to imagine (in some sense) a specific configuration of objects and properties. It is common to imagine situations in considerable detail, and this imagination is often accompanied by interpretation and reasoning. When one imagines a situation and reasons about it, the object of one's imagination is often revealed as a situation in which S is the case, for some S. When this is so, we can say that the imagined situation *verifies* S, and that one has *imagined that* S.[15]

Suppose all concede that Zoe is negatively conceivable. Is there reason to think that she eludes positive conceivability, or imaginability? Kriegel seems to think not. He says of Zoe that, "it seems to me perfectly possible to imagine such an inner life, even to imagine it from the first-person perspective – to imagine, that is, that it is my own inner life."[16] This last bit is important. According to Kriegel it is not as if we just imagine some person in the room with us and stipulate various truths about her inner life. Rather, we enter into her inner life and positively flesh it out for ourselves in our imagination, just as one might redeploy an imaginative capacity acquired by feeling an itch on one's right elbow in imagining what it is like to feel an itch on one's left elbow.

It is important for Kriegel's project that positive imagination is not stipulated to be imagination grounded in sensory imagery. Chalmers explicitly does not. However, in motivating the claim that total phenomenal states like the ones Zoe is supposed to enjoy are not positively imaginable, Pautz only considers attempts that do involve sensory imagery and then notes that they fall short. One might add a restriction to Chalmers' characterization of positive imagining, one that requires positive imagination to be grounded in sensory imagery. But this seems like an illegitimate move in the present context, since arguably imagining purely cognitive phenomenal states – especially from the inside – will not involve forming sensory imagery of them.

Pautz might concede that Zoe is indeed positively imaginable after all, but deny that what one positively imagines when one positively imagines her is a person who has phenomenal states. Recall that Kriegel presented Zoe to us in three stages: we consider various partial zombies, we synthesize a sensory-algedonic-emotional zombie from them, and then we stipulate that this person spends her time doing math. Pautz can accept all that. But then there is the further claim that the person imagined in this way has phenomenal states. This is an additional claim about the situation, not directly built into the three stages that help us to imagine the situation. In Chalmers' terms, Kriegel's claim is that the situation he has helped us to imagine in three stages is one that *verifies* the claim that the person in it has phenomenal states. This claim about what the imagined situation verifies is additional and Pautz might very well deny it.

Kriegel's claim that Zoe has phenomenal states depends on recognizing a phenomenal contrast between the case in which she fails to suddenly realize a mathematical truth and the case in which she succeeds in suddenly realizing a mathematical truth. The claim that there is such a contrast, however, is not compulsory. I notice phenomenal contrasts of this sort in my own life.

But I am not a sensory-algedonic-emotional zombie. Pautz might press the worry that reasoning from the existence of a phenomenal contrast in actual cases to the existence of a phenomenal contrast in hypothetical cases of sensory-algedonic-emotional zombies is illegitimate.

This is not how Kriegel reasons, however. As mentioned above he gives an argument that the contrast associated with Zoe's realization is phenomenal. The argument has two key premises. First, a mental state is phenomenal if it gives a rationally warranted appearance of an explanatory gap with physical states.[17] Second, Zoe's realization gives a rationally warranted appearance of an explanatory gap with physical states: "It is entirely natural to be deeply puzzled about how this episode could just be nothing but the vibrations of so many neurons inside the darkness of the skull."[18] I doubt that these considerations give us *independent* reason to believe the contrast associated with Zoe's realization is phenomenal. Suppose Kriegel's first premise is true. It does not follow that we can gain independent reason to think that a state is phenomenal by gaining reason to think it gives an appearance of an explanatory gap. In fact, the opposite seems to be the case: if a state gives an appearance of an explanatory gap it is typically because I can point to its phenomenal features and wonder to myself how anything like that could just be nothing but the vibrations of so many neurons. So there is a lacuna in Kriegel's reasoning: even if giving the appearance of an explanatory gap is a sufficient condition for being a phenomenal state, it does not follow that we can detect its presence independently of a prior detection of phenom- enology. This worry is particularly pressing when one takes into account a complication Kriegel himself raises: there are lots of explanatory gaps and many of them have nothing to do with phenomenology. I myself find it difficult to see how intentional states, regardless of whatever phenomenal features they might have, could just be nothing but the vibrations of so many neurons. So not only must we have reason to think the contrast associated with Zoe's realization gives an appearance of an explanatory gap, but we must have reason to think it is the right sort of explanatory gap. It seems to me that if we have such a reason, then it is just because we already have reason to think the contrast associated with Zoe's realization is phenomenal.

At this point it is not clear how to adjudicate the dispute. Suppose that in general if you set out to imagine an F you can tell whether you succeed. It doesn't follow that in general if you set out to imagine an F you can tell whether what you have imagined is also a G. Figuring out whether what you have imagined is also a G might require more resources than figuring out whether you have succeeded in imagining an F. I'm inclined to think that we are in this sort of situation. One might be confident that one has succeeded in imagining Zoe according to Kriegel's specifications. But one might doubt whether what one has imagined is someone with phenomenal states. Suppose Kriegel adds to his specification that Zoe must have phenomenal states. That is, suppose he does not argue for this using a phenomenal contrast, but builds it into the rules for counting as imagining Zoe. Then one might – with Pautz – lose one's confidence that one can succeed in imagining Zoe according to the new specifications. For the specifications would be tantamount to the request to imagine a total phenomenal state that includes cognitive phenomenal states but does not include any sensory phenomenal states. This is precisely what Pautz denies being able to do.

Glossed phenomenal contrast arguments

The phenomenal contrast argument that I will develop in this section is based on the example of "seeing" – or intuiting – a mathematical truth from the introduction. Here are the two cases:

> Case 1: You entertain the proposition that if $a < 1$, then $2 - 2a > 0$ and do not "see" that it is true. In particular you do not "see" how a's being less than 1 makes $2a$ smaller than 2 and so $2 - 2a$ greater than 0.

> Case 2: You entertain the proposition that if $a < 1$, then $2 - 2a > 0$ and do "see" that it is true. In particular you do "see" how a's being less than 1 makes $2a$ smaller than 2 and so $2 - 2a$ greater than 0.

Here is the phenomenal contrast argument:

(1)   Case 1 and Case 2 contain different phenomenal states.
(2)   The difference consists, at least in part, in this: in Case 2 but not in Case 1 you are in a phenomenal state P that makes you seem to be aware of an abstract state of affairs.
(3)   No possible combination of wholly sensory states puts one in P.
(4)   Some cognitive state – e.g. the state of intuiting that occurs in Case 2 – puts one in P.
(5)   Some cognitive states put one in a phenomenal state for which no wholly sensory states suffice – i.e. Irreducibility is true.

The argument is valid: (1) through (4) do logically imply (5). So the only question is whether all the premises are true. I will say something in support of each.

Premise (1) should be evident from one's own experience. There just is some phenomenal difference between "seeing" and not "seeing" a simple mathematical truth such as that if $a < 1$, then $2 - 2a > 0$.

Premise (2) is an added gloss on the nature of that phenomenal difference. This is what makes the argument a glossed phenomenal contrast argument. Neither pure nor hypothetical phenomenal contrast arguments depend on premises describing the phenomenal differences between contrasting cases. Glossed phenomenal contrast arguments do. This buys argumentative power at the cost of dialectical leverage. Whether the benefits outweigh the costs depends on how defensible the gloss is.

Let us distinguish three ways of defending the gloss in premise (2).

First, one might argue that it is immediately justified by introspection. Despite the reservations about introspection reviewed in the previous chapter, it is clear that some descriptions of phenomenal states are immediately justified by introspection.[19] Suppose you have a sharp headache. Suppose you make the following claims about it: "My headache is sharp," "My headache is not dull," "My headache does not feel like an itch on my elbow." How might you defend these claims? It seems perfectly reasonable to say in their defense that they are immediately justified by introspection. Such justification need not be very strong. Suppose you say: "My headache feels sharpest above my right eye, dulls over the bridge of my nose, and doesn't extend over my left eye." Maybe this claim is immediately justified by introspection, but if so, it is likely less justified than the claim that your headache does not feel like an itch on your elbow. In my view I have at least some immediate introspective justification for the gloss in premise (2). That said, I do not want to put too much weight on it.

Second, one might argue that the gloss best explains similarities between the phenomenal states it describes and other phenomenal states. Consider the following two cases:

Case 3: You entertain the proposition that there is mail in your mailbox but do not see that it is true. In particular, you do not look in your mailbox and see the mail sitting there.

Case 4: You entertain the proposition that there is mail in your mailbox and do see that it is true. In particular, you do look in your mailbox and see the mail sitting there.

Case 3 and Case 4 contain different phenomenal states. Many philosophers would agree that the difference consists, at least in part, in this: in Case 4 but not in Case 3 you are in a phenomenal state P* that makes you seem to be aware (in particular visually aware) of a concrete state of affairs (in particular the state of your mail sitting in your mailbox). I think that phenomenal state P in Case 2 and phenomenal state P* in Case 4 are similar in at least some respects. Further, I think that the gloss in (2) best captures these respects. For note that the similarity is not with respect to their content: mail and numbers are rather different. The similarity is with respect to their structure: both make you seem to be aware of a state of affairs that bears on the truth of a proposition you consider. Since in Case 2 the proposition is about abstract matters, the state of affairs you seem to be aware of in P is an abstract one.

One might worry that some other gloss better explains the similarities. And this brings us to the third way of supporting the gloss in premise (2): one might build up a case for it by arguing that it does better than various natural rivals.

Let us consider a few. I will divide them into two classes. The first class consists of rival glosses that do not involve apparent grasp of a truth. Examples include: P just consists in a relief of general tension; P just consists in a general feeling of getting it; P just consists a feeling of self-satisfaction – etc. The second class consists of glosses that replace apparent grasp of a truth via awareness with some other way of apparently grasping a truth. Examples include: P just makes the proposition that if $a < 1$, then $2 - 2a > 0$ seem true; P just casts the proposition that if $a < 1$, then $2 - 2a > 0$ in some favorable light – etc.

Rival glosses in the first class are open to the general worry that they fail to explain the similarities between P (the phenomenal state in Case 2) and P* (the phenomenal state in Case 4). Individual glosses in this class can be challenged by considering a case where a phenomenal state for which the rival gloss seems adequate occurs, and contrasting it with P. Consider relief of general tension. Even if P does include a relief of general tension, that is not all it consists in. Suppose you are rather tense while considering our example proposition. You don't "see" that it is true. But a pill that you took earlier kicks in and relieves your general tension. Now you feel the relief of general tension but still don't "see" that the proposition is true. In this case you are not in the same phenomenal state you are in when P occurs. Consider a general feeling of getting it. Even if P does include a general feeling of getting it, that is not all it consists in. Suppose someone tells you a joke and at first you don't get it. Then you do. This gives you a general feeling of getting it, but it doesn't make you "see" that if $a < 1$, then $2 - 2a > 0$. In this case you are not in the same phenomenal state you are in when P occurs. Making the joke a mathematical joke does not help. Here is an example:

> Three statisticians go out hunting together. After a while they spot a solitary rabbit. The first statistician takes aim and overshoots. The second aims and undershoots. The third shouts out "We got him![20]

Getting this joke puts you in a phenomenal state, but it is not the same phenomenal state you are in when P occurs. One might reply on behalf of this rival gloss that P consists of a somewhat more specific feeling of getting it, one that differentiates P from states that have nothing to do with the proposition that if $a < 1$, then $2 - 2a > 0$. For example maybe P consists of a feeling of getting it directed at an inner verbalization of "if $a < 1$, then $2 - 2a > 0$." Perhaps this does better. But it still seems to me to fall short of making clear the similarities between P and P*. Consider, for example, a feeling of getting it directed at an inner verbalization of "there is mail in my mailbox." That does not capture what it is like to see that there is mail in your mailbox.

Rival glosses in the second class are more plausible. If there is any gloss that might fit P better than the gloss in premise (2) it is that P just implies that the proposition that if $a < 1$, then $2 - 2a > 0$ seems true. It could be that even if we replace the gloss in (2) with this gloss premise (3) will remain true. In that case the glossed phenomenal contrast will remain sound. My own case for (3), however, will exploit special features of seeming awareness. So I do want to insist that P is special in that it implies seeming awareness of an abstract state of affairs – rather like Augustine's third kind of vision described in the quote that opens this book.

Motivation for this derives from consideration of another mathematical claim:

> Every even number greater than 2 is the sum of two primes.

This is Goldbach's Conjecture. It remains unproved. It is difficult to shake the feeling that it is true, however. This is especially so if you go through a bunch of examples: you try $4 = 2 + 2$, $6 = 3 + 3$, $8 = 3 + 5$, $10 = 5 + 5$, $12 = 5 + 7$, etc. After a while the proposition just seems true. Even so,

I maintain: you never get that sense of being aware of the abstract state of affairs that makes it true. No matter how intense the seeming to be true, it is not grounded in any apparent awareness of how the structure of the evens and the structure of the primes link up so as to make the proposition true. Contrast the proposition that if $a < 1$, then $2 - 2a > 0$. Here you do get a sense of being aware of the ground of the proposition's truth. The relevant structure seems present to mind in a way that it isn't for Goldbach's Conjecture.

The gloss according to which P just implies that the proposition that if $a < 1$, then $2 - 2a > 0$ seems true also fails to explain the similarity between P in Case 2, when you have the intuition, and P* in Case 4, when you see the mail. Suppose while considering the proposition that there is mail in your mailbox you come to have a premonition that it is true. Suppose this premonition is very intense. This is more like the case of Goldbach's Conjecture. But it is not like the case of "seeing" that if $a < 1$, then $2 - 2a > 0$. In that case you do not have an experience like an intense premonition. Your experience is more like seeing the mail in the mailbox. One final note about this, however, is that my claim here is metaphysically non-committal: for all I have said there might be no mathematical states of affairs. My claim is about what your experience feels like, not about its veridicality. Even nominalists about mathematics tend to admit that Platonism captures the appearances.

Premise (3) depends on the nature of wholly sensory states. Wholly sensory states include states of awareness or states akin to awareness directed at one's spatiotemporal vicinity. If my gloss on the phenomenal state P is correct, however, then it implies seeming awareness of an abstract state of affairs – one that is non-spatiotemporal. One might press a bold view of high-level perception according to which wholly sensory states have representational contents that are about abstract states of affairs. I think this is implausible, but I can concede it for the sake of argument here. What I deny is that wholly sensory states might make one or seem to make one aware of abstract states of affairs. Just representing a state of affairs is one thing. Seeming to stand in an awareness relation to a state of affairs is something over and above that: in the case of seeming awareness the state of affairs is felt to be there before one's mind and a candidate for demonstrative thought. What I'm denying is that a wholly sensory state can give you this sense with respect to abstract states of affairs.

Premise (4) is motivated by the phenomenal contrast case and the nature of cognitive states. The phenomenal contrast case shows that some state or other does put one in the phenomenal state P. And there is nothing in the nature of cognitive states that rules out the possibility of a cognitive state putting one in P. These two observations together remove any obstacle to accepting the prima facie plausible view that one's cognitive state of intuiting that if $a < 1$, then $2 - 2a > 0$ puts one in P.

So these are my reasons for accepting the premises in the argument. If they are true, then so is the conclusion, i.e. so is Irreducibility.

Notes

1 Koksvik 2011 also draws a distinction between ostensive and argumentative uses of phenomenal contrasts.
2 Strawson 1994, 5–6.
3 See, for example, Carruthers and Veillet 2011, Levine 2011, Prinz 2011, and Tye and Wright 2011.
4 This is taken from Burton 2008, 5.
5 See, for example, Pitt 2004, Horgan and Tienson 2002, and Siewert 1998, 2011.
6 For discussion see Siegel 2006c, 2010 and the papers in Hawley and Macpherson 2011.
7 See, for example, O'Callaghan 2011. O'Callaghan gives reasons for doubting that the understanding is high-level perception of semantic properties. But he also gives reasons for thinking there are wholly sensory states that can account for the phenomenal contrast between Jacques and Jack. So the impact on the phenomenal contrast argument is mixed.
8 The example is from Siewert 1998, 276–277.
9 The argument is in Kriegel forthcoming.
10 See Horgan 2011, 60.
11 Kriegel forthcoming.
12 Ibid.
13 Ibid.
14 Pautz 2013, 219.
15 Chalmers 2002a, 149–150. See also Yablo 1993.
16 Kriegel forthcoming.
17 Section 3 of Kriegel (forthcoming) elaborates and defends this premise. My formulation does not exactly match Kriegel's, but the basic idea is the same and differences in detail will not matter here.
18 Kriegel forthcoming.
19 Siewert 2012 is an illuminating discussion of this phenomenon.

20 From Walter Hickey, "13 Jokes That Every Math Geek Will Find Hilarious," *Business Insider*, 21 May 2013, http://www.businessinsider.com/13-math-jokes-that-every-mathematician-finds-absolutely-hilarious-2013-5

Further reading

Siegel (2010) discusses the method of phenomenal contrast. Strawson (1994), Siewert (1998, 2011), Horgan and Tienson (2002), Pitt (2004), and Kriegel (forthcoming) defend applications of it to cognitive phenomenology. Carruthers and Veillet (2011), Levine (2011), Prinz (2011), and Tye and Wright (2011) criticize these applications.

3

VALUE

According to Mill "pleasure, and freedom from pain, are the only things desirable as ends." This does not imply that the good life is a degrading one, fit for swine, however, at least partly because there are "pleasures of the intellect, of the feelings and imagination, and of the moral sentiments," which possess "a much higher value as pleasures" than those of "mere sensation." These are familiar aspects of Mill's theory of value.[1]

Someone interested in defending the view that there is irreducible cognitive phenomenology might find some encouragement here. Suppose the pleasure afforded by an experience depends on its phenomenology. And suppose Mill is right that "mere sensation" cannot afford the same pleasures as "the intellect." Then, it would seem, there must be phenomenology associated with intellectual experiences grounding the "higher" pleasures they provide, which is distinct from the phenomenology associated with sensory experiences grounding the "lower" pleasures they provide.

The argument is unsatisfactory in its present form. But it serves to illustrate the kind of argument that is my concern in this chapter. Put generally, arguments of this kind start from reflections on value and conclude with the claim that there is irreducible cognitive phenomenology – that Irreducibility is true. My aim is to explore the prospects of such arguments. The results of this exploration are mixed. Some of the arguments fail and some succeed but only at the cost of dialectical ineffectuality. There is at least one argument, however, that I believe is both sound and dialectically satisfactory. In my view the failures are as illuminating as the successes: the interest of the project is not so much that it will result in a proof that there is irreducible cognitive phenomenology, but that it will shed light on some of the connections between value, phenomenology, and conscious thought.

Here is the plan. In the first section ("Phenomenal Value"), I discuss the relationship between phenomenology and value. In the second ("The Argument from Interestingness"), I consider Strawson's argument from interestingness, which I take to be an example of an argument from reflection on value for irreducible cognitive phenomenology. I suggest there is a gap in Strawson's argument and I propose a way of closing this gap. The strategy is to focus on the Millian idea that some cognitive states differ in value from all sensory states. In the third section ("Differences in Value"), I clarify how I understand this claim. And in the fourth ("Supporting the Difference in Value Premise"), I develop and assess two ways of supporting it.

Phenomenal value

Suppose you spot a lion running your way. This is a mental state. It is valuable because it alerts you to a present danger. This is an example of a mental state having instrumental value. A mental state's instrumental value is the value it has in virtue of the ends it serves.

Suppose you witness a great historical event – e.g. a significant speech, a record-breaking achievement, or a progressive victory. This is a mental state. It might have some instrumental value, for now you have a story to tell your friends. But what makes the story worth telling? Plausibly it is because witnessing a great historical event is itself valuable. This is sometimes called intrinsic or final value. A mental state's final value is the value it has for its own sake.

Spotting a lion running your way and witnessing a great historical event are phenomenally conscious mental states. Is there any reason to think that in addition to the values already pointed out they have value in virtue of their phenomenal characters? We might call this their phenomenal value. Another way to raise the issue of phenomenal value is to consider the final value of phenomenal states. Spotting a lion on an occasion puts you in some phenomenal state. Witnessing a particular great historical event puts you in some phenomenal state. Is there any reason to think that the phenomenal states themselves have final value? A mental state has phenomenal value just in case it puts you in a phenomenal state that has final value. These are just two ways of getting at the same issue, though it is useful to have both.

Siewert considers the question of phenomenal value in *The Significance of Consciousness*. According to Siewert, "we can see that we value the possession of phenomenal features for its own sake, if only we can see that we do not value this merely for the sake of someone's or something's having non-phenomenal features."[2] Take spotting a lion running your way. When you spot a lion running your way you have some valuable "nonphenomenal features": you are alerted to a present danger for example. Plausibly, you also have some valuable "phenomenal features," i.e. are in some valuable phenomenal states. I imagine there is something impressive in the visual experience itself for example. Now ask yourself: is the visual phenomenal state associated with spotting a lion valuable just because it is also associated with various non-phenomenal states such as being alerted to a present danger? Plausibly the answer is no. The association with non-phenomenal states is important. But it is not the sole ground of the value realized by the visual phenomenal state. If this is so, then the visual phenomenal state has final value. In other words, spotting a lion running your way is a mental state with some phenomenal value in addition to various other values.

Siewert also considers cognitive states. He gives an example close to one we will explore in some detail below:

> Suppose you like thinking about mathematics. Would it suit you just as well (or even better) if you always got the same valuable results as you get from conscious mathematical thinking, but *without* the conscious thinking? Is it all the same to you if you always acquire the ability to produce a proof or the solution to a problem so as to write this out, and actually express these conclusions, *only while totally devoid of conscious thought?* I imagine no one who likes mathematics would be just as satisfied doing it only while in some zombie-ish state, any more than one who likes sex would just as soon have a zombified sex life.[3]

Siewert's assessment seems plausible. One might wonder whether it provides grounds for endorsing Irreducibility. Siewert does not say it does. His arguments for irreducible cognitive phenomenology occur earlier in *The Significance of Consciousness*. Still, one might wonder whether his observation about the value of conscious thought can be worked into an additional argument for cognitive phenomenology.

I do not think that it can be. Suppose zombie mathematical cognition is not as valuable as conscious mathematical cognition. So conscious mathematical cognition has some phenomenal value. Still, it could be that the phenomenal value resides in the final value of sensory phenomenal states associated with mathematical cognition – e.g. visualizing, verbalizing, etc. Nothing in the observation that conscious mathematical cognition has some phenomenal value rules this possibility out. It is one thing to be in a mental state that is both phenomenally valuable and cognitive. It is another thing to be in a mental state that is phenomenally valuable in a way that is unique to cognition.

The argument from interestingness

Consider an argument Galen Strawson gives in a recent paper, "Cognitive Phenomenology: Real Life," which he calls "the argument from interestingness":

> Premise 1: If cognitive experience didn't exist, life – experience – would be pretty boring.
> Premise 2: Life – experience – is intricately and complexly interesting and various.
> Conclusion: cognitive experience exists.[4]

Strawson allows that there might be "interestedness-feelings" that are caused by various occurrences in our lives. But without "cognitive experience" this falls short of accounting for the phenomena supporting Premise 2. His explanation of why is illuminating. It is:

> Because *we never consciously grasp or entertain the meaning of anything.* Instead, we (a) non-consciously and sub-experientially register some conceptual content, in a way that is, on the no-cognitive-experience view, and so far as phenomenological goings-on are concerned, no different from the way in which machines can be said to register conceptual content. This then causes in us (b) a certain sort of sense/feeling experience, a certain quantum of interestedness-feeling, say – experience which involves no experience of the specific content of the registered content.[5]

Notice, however, that Strawson takes the denial of "cognitive experience" to imply the denial of phenomenally conscious cognitive states such as states of consciously understanding some utterance – i.e. to imply the denial of the thesis I called Phenomenal Presence. So he is not using "cognitive experience" in the way that I am using "irreducible cognitive phenomenology." These are technical terms, and their usage is open to stipulation. But I believe that focusing the debate on irreducible cognitive phenomenology, i.e. Irreducibility, rather than phenomenally conscious cognitive states, i.e. Phenomenal Presence, is preferable. The reason is one Strawson should find congenial: denying Phenomenal Presence is just incredible.[6] Though I believe that philosophers who deny the existence of irreducible cognitive phenomenology are mistaken, I do not think that they are subscribing to the incredible view that denies the existence of phenomenally conscious cognitive states. There is a better way to make sense of what they are denying, namely Irreducibility.[7]

Can Strawson's argument from interestingness support Irreducibility? It isn't clear. Suppose phenomenally conscious cognitive states suffice to make life intricately interesting and various, but their phenomenal characters are ones that phenomenally conscious wholly sensory states could have – i.e. the phenomenal states they put one in are ones that some phenomenally conscious wholly sensory states might put one in. Then the answer is that Strawson's argument does not support believing Irreducibility.

One way to close the gap between the sorts of considerations Strawson brings up and Irreducibility is to focus on differences in ways of being interesting or more generally differences in ways of being valuable. Suppose cognitive states are valuable in ways that are both grounded in their phenomenal character and couldn't be duplicated by sensory states. Then we would have reason to believe Irreducibility: there would have to be cognitive phenomenal states to ground these distinctively cognitive phenomenal values.

We can make this argument more explicit as follows:

(1) Some conscious cognitive states have a phenomenal value that every wholly sensory state lacks.
(2) Whatever difference in phenomenal value there is between two phenomenally conscious states is grounded in differences in what phenomenal states they put one in.
(3) So, some cognitive states put one in phenomenal states for which no wholly sensory states suffice – i.e. Irreducibility is true.

Premise (2) is true in virtue of the meaning of "phenomenal value." The conclusion (3) clearly follows from (1) and (2). Premise (1) is doing all the substantive work. Let's call it the Difference in Value Premise. The next section is about what it means. The section after explores ways of supporting it.

Differences in value

The aim of this section is to clarify how I will understand claims about difference in value such as the Difference in Value Premise.

I need not assume any particular theory of value. Something is valuable just in case it has properties that make adopting some positive evaluative attitude or stance – e.g. desiring, respecting, admiring, loving, caring for, choosing, enjoying, promoting, protecting, etc. – toward it appropriate. According to "fitting attitude" theories of value this schema can be used to explain the nature of value.[8] But I am simply using it to help locate the relevant notion. It could be that value is basic and what makes an attitude or stance count as a positive evaluative attitude or stance is that bearing it to something is appropriate just in case that thing realizes some value – e.g. pleasure, knowledge, achievement, beauty, virtue, friendship, justice, freedom, equality, etc. I believe I can remain neutral on this and most other controversial issues about the nature of value. I will assume that claims about value are true or false (or in some other way correct or incorrect) and that reflection can enable us to tell which is the case. These are minimal assumptions one must make in order to appeal to claims about value in arguments at all.

Claims about differences in value can be understood in at least three different ways. Consider the following:

(A) Giving 10 dollars to charity is better than giving 5 dollars to charity.
(B) The value of a legal career and the value of a musical career cannot be compared.
(C) Developing friendships and pursuing an education are valuable in different ways.

All of these are claims about difference in value. But they differ in what they mean. Claim (A) is a comparative value judgment. Claim (B) is a claim about the impossibility of making a true comparative value judgment such as the one made in (A).[9] And claim (C) is a claim about the plurality of values. Two clarifications about (C) are in order. First, claim (C) does not imply a claim such as the one made in (B): perhaps developing friendships is better than pursuing an education, or perhaps the opposite is true, or perhaps, as is more likely, some more nuanced comparative value judgment is true.[10] Second, claim (C) need not rule out a monistic theory of ultimate value: perhaps, as hedonists think, pleasure is the ultimate value, and developing friendships and pursuing an education are valuable because of the pleasures they afford, but differ in the ways they afford these pleasures.[11]

I will interpret the Difference in Value Premise as making a claim like (C) – i.e. a claim about the plurality of values. Maybe certain cognitive states are greater in value than any sensory states. Maybe the two sorts of states cannot be compared. Both claims are compatible with the Difference in Value Premise, but neither is implied by it.

Supporting the Difference in Value Premise

The Difference in Value Premise tells us that some cognitive states have a phenomenal value that every wholly sensory state lacks. Let us consider a particular cognitive state. If the particular cognitive state is a cognitive state with phenomenal value that every wholly sensory state lacks, then the general Difference in Value Premise will be true.

I will use a simple mathematical example. Look at the following diagram and consider the proposition that $(a + b)^2 \geq 4ab$.

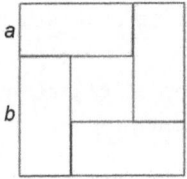

There are a number of mental states that this exercise might put you in. There is a sensory state of seeing the diagram. There is a cognitive state of intuiting the truth of the proposition that $(a + b)^2 \geq 4ab$. I want to focus on a different mental state one might be in. There is something charming or pleasant about the way the diagram illustrates the algebraic truth. This is something one might appreciate. And doing so is being in a certain mental state. I'll refer to the pattern of reasoning that supports the algebraic truth via reflections on the diagram as "the proof." This is the thing that is charming or pleasant. I'll refer to the state of appreciating its charm as "the state of appreciating the charm of the proof" or sometimes "the state of appreciating the proof" for short. I think this is about as good a candidate as any for a cognitive state with phenomenal value that every wholly sensory state lacks.[12]

I will consider two ways of motivating the claim that the state of appreciating the charm of the proof has phenomenal value that every wholly sensory state lacks. The first way seems to me sound but dialectically weak. The second way seems to me both sound and dialectically satisfactory.

Rational regret

In the *Nicomachean Ethics*, Aristotle asks us to, "[s]uppose, for instance, a tyrant tells you to do something shameful, when he has control over your parents and children, and if you do it, they will live, but if not, they will die."[13] About this case, Michael Stocker writes:

> In Aristotle's case, if the man rescues his family, he gives up his honor, and if he saves his honor, he gives up his family. And even if he clearly sees that he must save his family, and thus that he must give up his honor, he can regret the loss of his honor. The loss of his honor is regrettable even if losing it is entirely justified, perhaps obligatory. So too, of course, losing one's family would be regrettable, even if justified or obligatory.
>
> In these conflicts, there is a strong, evaluative reason to do each conflicting act rather than the other. This goes beyond saying that each incompossible act has value. After all, choosing each dish of ice cream has value. But this does not give one any reason to choose a lesser or an equal dish rather than the other. The point here is one about monism, not simply about trivial choices. If the very same value will be achieved by doing each of the incompossible acts, there seems no evaluative reason to do one act rather than the other, unless it is better than the other ... [14]

The idea is that the value of honor and the value of family are different because in possessing one you do not recover the value lost in forgoing the other. This is shown by the rationality of regret. Suppose you choose to save your family. Even if this is your best option, it might be rational for you to regret losing honor. But regret wouldn't be rational if there were no value you are missing. So there is some value you are missing, one not provided by your family, however valuable your family might be.

We can imagine a similar case that bears on our present concerns. Suppose a tyrant/mad scientist tells you that he is taking over your brain, but you can now make a choice about which course of phenomenally conscious states you will be in. Either you can have a course that includes the state of appreciating the charm of the proof. Or you can have a course that only includes wholly sensory states. This course of states might include states of taking pleasure in the words and pictures in the presentation of the proof. But this is different from appreciating the charm of the proof. The proof is an abstract pattern of reasoning. Even if the words and pictures are themselves charming, appreciating their charm is not the same as appreciating the charm of the proof. Suppose you do choose the option of having only wholly sensory states. This might be your best option because the sensory states might be rather fantastic. Still, it seems, you could rationally regret forgoing the state of appreciating the charm of the proof. And just as with Aristotle's case, there must be a missing value, one not recovered by the course of sensory states you will have, which value makes regret rational.

We can put the argument like this:

(1)   It is rational to regret choosing the phenomenal states the course of wholly sensory states puts one in over the phenomenal states the state of appreciating the charm of the proof puts one in.
(2)   If it is rational to regret choosing the phenomenal states the course of wholly sensory states puts one in over the phenomenal states the state of appreciating the charm of the proof puts one in, then this is because the state of appreciating the charm of the proof has a phenomenal value that wholly sensory states lack.
(3)   So the state of appreciating the charm of the proof has a phenomenal value that wholly sensory states lack.

The argument is valid. And I think its premises are true. But the argument is dialectically weak.

In particular: if one took oneself to have reason to deny Irreducibility, which is the conclusion we are aiming to support eventually, then one should take oneself to have reason to deny premise (1), which I will call the Rational Regret Premise. One should concede that a believer in irreducible cognitive phenomenology might *feel* regret in the imagined situation. But one should deny that it is *rational* regret, grounded in a genuinely forgone phenomenal value. The feeling might be irrational. And nothing in the argument itself establishes that it is not.

Not all good arguments are dialectically useful. Sometimes an argument is good because it makes the interconnections among one's own commitments clearer, or increases one's own level of justification for a belief, even if the argumentative route to that increase is not available from every reasonable starting point. So the argument from the Difference in Value Premise to Irreducibility still has some interest even if it is based on considerations about rational regret that are only available to someone who already believes in irreducible cognitive phenomenology. That said, since there is a dispute about irreducible cognitive phenomenology in the literature that needs resolving, it will be worth exploring the prospects of another potentially dialectically more satisfactory form of argument.

Differences in valuing

Elizabeth Anderson summarizes her account of value as follows:

> I reduce "x is good" roughly to "it is rational to value x," where to value something is to adopt toward it a favorable attitude susceptible to rational reflection.[15]

This is a fitting attitude theory of value. As noted in the third section (p. 67), however, a schema of the sort Anderson endorses might be true even if it does not constitute a reduction. Further, it only needs to be true for consequences of it to be true as well. It is one of the consequences that Anderson draws from the schema that I am interested in here:

> My theory says that there are many kinds of intrinsic value, because it makes sense for us to value people intrinsically in many ways, such as by love, respect, honor, awe, and admiration. Some of these attitudes vary by degrees, so it makes sense to shade our expressions of these attitudes to the degree to which they are merited. If a critic judges one musician to be more admirable than another, it may make sense for her to praise the more admirable one more highly or more enthusiastically. So some kinds of intrinsic value do vary by degrees.
>   But little sense can be made of adding different instances of intrinsic value. How do you add the admirability of a musician to the adorability of a puppy? No rational attitude or action takes such a notional sum as its object.[16]

Behind the point about additivity, which I set aside, is a point about plurality, which is my focus. The value of a musician is different from the value of a puppy, and one consideration that shows this is that whereas valuing the musician involves admiring the musician, valuing the puppy does not, but rather involves finding the puppy adorable.

This suggests a general claim: if there is a way of valuing X that is not a way of valuing Y, then X has a value that Y lacks. The idea is that given the coordination of values and valuing, things with the same values should be objects of the same forms of valuing, so if different forms of valuing fit them, this is evidence of different values.

One might have the following worry.[17] Valuing ice cream during the week is different from valuing ice cream during the weekend, but the value of ice cream remains the same. There are two ways to resist the potential counter-example. First, one might agree that there are different ways of valuing ice cream in play, but one might insist that ice cream during the week realizes different values from ice cream during the weekend. During the week it relieves stress; during the weekend it increases enjoyment. Second, one might resist the idea that there are two different ways of valuing ice cream in play: there is one way of valuing ice cream in play, and it just occurs at different points in the week. This second reply depends on individuating ways of valuing less finely than descriptions of ways of valuing. This strikes me as a plausible commitment, however, one supported by our very impression that ice cream does not demand different forms of valuing it at different points in the week.

The coordination between values and valuing suggests another argument that the state of appreciating the charm of the proof has a value that every wholly sensory state lacks:

(1) There is a way of valuing the phenomenal states the state of appreciating the charm of the proof puts one in that is not a way of valuing the phenomenal states any wholly sensory states put one in.

(2) If there is a way of valuing X that is not a way of valuing Y, then X has a value that Y lacks.

(3) So the state of appreciating the charm of the proof has a phenomenal value that wholly sensory states lack.

Once again the argument is valid. And I think its premises are true. In this case, it also seems to me that the argument is dialectically effective.

In particular it seems to me that premise (1), which I will call the Difference in Valuing Premise, can be supported in a dialectically more effective way than was available for supporting the Rational Regret Premise. There are two preliminary points to make.

First, I am not claiming that there are no ways of valuing the phenomenal states grounded in the state of appreciating the proof that are also ways of valuing the phenomenal states grounded in some wholly sensory states. Presumably there are. If you value some phenomenal state, then, plausibly, you will seek to be in phenomenally conscious states that put you in it and you will recommend such states to others. This sort of valuing does not distinguish between the different values realized by different phenomenal states. We might call it valuing by promoting. But we do not just promote the things we value. Sometimes we also savor them. If we want to find a difference in the values realized by different phenomenal states, then we should look to how we value them by savoring them, not by promoting them.

Second, though there is a distinction between savoring the objects presented to one in a phenomenal state and savoring the phenomenal state itself, the two are intimately related. According to some philosophers phenomenal states in general are "transparent." Michael Tye explains the thesis in a way that has a bearing on our present concerns:

> Here is one way of illustrating the thesis of transparency for the perceptual case: Suppose you are standing before a tapestry in an art gallery. As you take in the rich and varied colors of the cloth, you are told to pay close attention to your visual experience and its phenomenology. What do you do? Those who accept the transparency thesis say that you attend closely to the *tapestry* and details in it. You are aware of something outside you – the tapestry – and of various qualities that you experience as being qualities of parts of the tapestry, and by being aware of these things you are aware of what it is like for you subjectively or phenomenally.[18]

We need not commit to the claim that it is impossible to stand in an awareness relation to one's phenomenal states. But Tye is surely correct in pointing out that in the sort of scenario he describes, when we try to appreciate our phenomenal states what we do is we focus on how the objects they make us aware of, or at least seem to make us aware of, appear in them.[19] This bears on savoring as follows: by and large, savoring a phenomenal state consists in savoring how the object it makes you aware of, or seems to make you aware of, appears in it. This applies to phenomenal states presenting tapestries, wines, and proofs.

These two preliminary points in place, we can reason as follows. One way to value the phenomenal states grounded in the state of appreciating the charm of the proof is to savor how the proof they make you aware of, or seem to make you aware of, appears in them. Proofs are mathematical objects. So if a phenomenal state can be valued in the same ways as these, then it must make you aware of, or seem to make you aware of, a mathematical object. But no wholly sensory states make one aware of, or even seem to make one aware of, mathematical objects. So there is a way of valuing the phenomenal states grounded in the state of appreciating the proof that is not a way of valuing the phenomenal states grounded in any wholly sensory states. And that is just the Difference in Valuing Premise we aimed to support.

In my view the foregoing line of reasoning is both sound and dialectally stronger than that which one might pursue in favor of the Rational Regret Premise. Notice that even if one took oneself to have reasons to deny Irreducibility, still one might accept the premises in the line of reasoning supporting the Difference in Valuing Premise. Of course, if one took oneself to have reasons to deny Irreducibility one might *modus tollens* my *modus ponens*. But that is always an option. My point is that there is nothing in the reasoning in favor of the Difference in Valuing Premise that I have offered that obviously begs the question against opponents of Irreducibility. It might not be dialectically impregnable. But it is dialectically satisfactory.

There are three main points one might resist in the reasoning I have offered.

First, one might deny that there are any phenomenal states that make one aware of, or at least seem to make one aware of, the proof. One reply is that in the previous chapter I gave independent reasons for thinking some phenomenal states do at least seem to make one aware of mathematical states of affairs. It is not clear why seeming awareness of mathematical proofs should be regarded with more suspicion than seeming awareness of mathematical states of affairs. And here, again, I emphasize the "seeming" so as to sidestep worries about nominalism.

Further, there is another reply specific to the case at hand. The line of resistance under consideration is in conflict with a widely held belief about the nature of aesthetic appreciation. In the literature on aesthetics, philosophers discuss the "Acquaintance Principle," which "maintains that aesthetic knowledge must be acquired through first-hand experience of the object of knowledge and cannot be transmitted from person to person."[20] The point about transmission is controversial. What isn't controversial is that aesthetic experiences − e.g. states of appreciating the charm of something − are examples of the relevant acquaintance or first-hand experience. Since acquaintance or first-hand experience is, or at least includes, awareness, it follows that states of appreciating the charm of an object − including cases where that object is a proof − require awareness, or at least seeming awareness, of that object.

One might invoke the distinction between phenomenally conscious state and phenomenal state, and argue that the "Acquaintance Principle" only applies to the phenomenally conscious states of aesthetic appreciation, not the phenomenal states that these states put one in. But this entails that the phenomenal states themselves do not amount to, or even have the same structure as, aesthetic appreciation, and that is a large bullet to bite. It implies that a state cannot be both a state of aesthetic appreciation, even of a merely apparently existing thing, and phenomenally individuated. It is difficult to see what independent motivation there might be for such a view.

As a second line of resistance one might deny that the phenomenal states presenting the proof can be savored in the way that phenomenal states presenting a tapestry can be savored. This seems ad hoc. If Tye's considerations are cogent, and they do seem cogent when interpreted in the modest way that I have suggested, then it is entirely unmotivated to insist that they fail to apply across the board to all forms of savoring of phenomenal states, at least provided those phenomenal states are ones that present objects at all. Maybe there are raw feels and maybe they are an exception. But the phenomenal states involved in the state of appreciating the charm of the proof are not plausibly assimilated to raw feels.

Third, one might reject my assumption that wholly sensory states cannot make one aware of, or even seem to make one aware of, a mathematical object. This brings us back to the issue of high-level content. The fact that some philosophers think sensory states have high-level contents might encourage an opponent of Irreducibility to pursue the present line of resistance. My assumption that wholly sensory states cannot make one aware of, or even seem to make one aware of, a mathematical object is, however, compatible with a liberal view about the contents of sensory states. Suppose some sensory states have high-level contents to the effect that some words and pictures have a certain meaning, present a proof, and maybe even present a charming proof. Even if there were sensory states with such contents, it wouldn't follow that such states might make one aware of, or even seem to make one aware of, a mathematical object. This is because the content of a state is different from the objects it makes one aware of, or seems to make one aware of. Even if the content represents mathematical objects and properties, it does not follow that the state makes one aware of, or seems to make one aware of, a mathematical object. Consider a humdrum example. When you see that someone is happy by seeing their smile, maybe your visual state represents happiness, but it is not the case that you are or seem to stand in the visual awareness relation to happiness. You stand in the visual awareness relation to the smile, and in doing so you are in, we are supposing, a visual state that represents happiness. Similarly, even if you could see that some words and pictures present a proof, it is not the case that you are or seem to stand in the visual awareness relation to the proof. You stand in the seeing relation to the words and pictures, and in doing so you are in, we are supposing, a visual state that represents the property of presenting a proof. So high-level content views do not support this present line of resistance. And it is unclear what other support one might give to it.

Summary

I conclude that there is support for the Difference in Valuing Premise. Once this premise is in place, then we can put all of the foregoing together into one argument for Irreducibility:

(1)   There is a way of valuing the phenomenal states the state of appreciating the charm of the proof puts one in that is not a way of valuing the phenomenal states any wholly sensory states put one in. [Difference in Valuing Premise]

(2)   If there is a way of valuing X that is not a way of valuing Y, then X has a value that Y lacks.

(3)   So the state of appreciating the charm of the proof has a phenomenal value that wholly sensory states lack.

(4)   Some conscious cognitive states have a phenomenal value that every wholly sensory state lacks. [Difference in Value Premise]

(5)   Whatever difference in phenomenal value there is between two phenomenally conscious states is grounded in differences in what phenomenal states they put one in.

(6)   So, some cognitive states put one in phenomenal states for which no wholly sensory states suffice. [Irreducibility]

In my view this is a dialectically satisfactory argumentative route from reflections on value to the conclusion that there is irreducible cognitive phenomenology.

Notes

1 The relevant discussion, from which I have drawn the quoted phrases, occurs in Chapter 2 of *Utilitarianism*, 278–279 in Mill 1987.

2 Siewert 1998, 314.

3 Ibid., 324.

4 Strawson 2011, 299.

5 Ibid., 300.

6 See Ibid., 289–291.

7 This is a point Smithies 2013b makes clearly, and Carruthers and Veillet 2011, Levine 2011, Prinz 2011, Tye 2003, and Tye and Wright 2011 all explicitly distinguish claims like Phenomenal Presence from claims like Irreducibility and endorse the former while denying the latter.

8 For a helpful survey see Jacobson 2011.

9 See Raz 1986. The issue of whether this sort of claim about incomparability is ever true is a controversial one on which I will remain neutral. For further discussion, see Chang 1997.

10 For example: notable friendships are better than nominal educations and notable educations are better than nominal friendships. See Chang 1997, 14–16.

11 Plausibly this is Mill's view. See Mason 2011.

12 States of appreciating some aesthetic property (e.g. charm, beauty, elegance) of some mathematical object (e.g. definition, theorem, proof) are widely reported among mathematicians. A *locus classicus* is Hardy 1992. The relevant discussion runs from sections 10 to 18. Sinclair *et al.* (2006) contains a number of such reports and references to additional reports in the literature. The best way to convince oneself of the existence of such states is to experience being in one for oneself. I hope the example given in the text works. Toward the same end, Hardy presents a few simple proofs with commentary. Strawson (2011) also draws attention to these sorts of experiences in elaborating on his argument from interestingness.

13 Bk. 3, ch. 1 (cited in Stocker 1997, 199–200).

14 Stocker 1997, 199–200.

15 Anderson 1997, 95.

16 Ibid., 97.

17 Uriah Kriegel suggested it to me.

18 Tye 2009, 117.

19 I add "or at least seem to make us aware of" to take care of the case in which one appreciates one's hallucination of a tapestry by focusing on how the hallucinated tapestry is presented in it.

20 Budd 2003, 386.

Further reading

The inspiration for this chapter is Strawson's "argument from interesting-ness" presented in Strawson (2011). Chang (1997) is a useful place to start looking into questions about the plurality of values. Siewert (1998 and 2013) takes up general issues about the significance of phenomenal consciousness.

4

TIME

So far we have examined arguments for irreducible cognitive phenomenology. In this chapter and the next we will look at arguments against irreducible cognitive phenomenology.

The arguments in this chapter focus on a special class of conscious cognitive states, what I will call conscious thoughts. Conscious thoughts include judging, supposing, entertaining, recollecting, etc. The sudden realizations that Siewert and Kriegel discuss are examples of conscious thoughts. When you suddenly realize that you have an appointment, you have a conscious thought. When – in the context of working out a proof – you suddenly realize that any number not on some supposed finite list of primes must be composite and so divisible by some number on the list, you have a conscious thought.

Conscious thoughts are conscious cognitive states with the structure of a propositional attitude. Propositional attitudes have two aspects. One aspect is the propositional content. This is the sort of thing picked out by a "that" clause such as "that you have an appointment." Propositional contents are true or false relative to different ways the world could be.[1] The second aspect is the attitude. This is the sort of thing picked out by verbs such as "suddenly realize," which take "that" clauses as complements. Attitudes are associated with psychological roles: sudden realizations play a role in psychological explanation that is different from the roles played by desires, fears, suppositions, etc. Each propositional attitude is a mental state that consists of bearing some attitude to some propositional content. And conscious thoughts are conscious cognitive states with just this structure.

Not all conscious cognitive states are conscious thoughts in this sense. Consider, for example, understanding the meaning of the kite passage, intuiting that if $a < 1$, then $2 - 2a > 0$, or reasoning through the whole proof that there is an infinite number of primes. Each of these mental states includes attitudes towards propositions. But they also include more. Understanding the meaning of the kite passage includes the mental states involved in reading. Intuiting that if $a < 1$, then $2 - 2a > 0$ includes apparent awareness of an abstract state of affairs. And reasoning through the whole proof that there is an infinite number of primes includes multiple interconnected propositional attitudes, such as supposing premises and judging logical relations.

This chapter is exclusively concerned with conscious thoughts. The reason for this is that conscious cognitive states in general exhibit a variety of temporal structures, and the arguments to be considered in this chapter aim to challenge Irreducibility on the basis of claims about the characteristic temporal structure of conscious thoughts narrowly construed. In particular they draw on certain criticisms Peter Geach pressed against William James. James argued that experiences, including conscious thoughts, flow in a stream of consciousness. Geach argued that whatever we say about other experiences, conscious thoughts at least do not flow, but rather occur in discrete sequences. The unifying theme of the group of arguments I consider in this chapter is the idea that Geach's criticisms of James are cogent and provide a basis for challenging Irreducibility, at least insofar as it applies to conscious thoughts narrowly construed.

The plan is this. In the first section, I take up preliminary matters. In the second ("The Stream of Consiousness"), I explore James's view that consciousness flows in a stream. There are a number of different theses that might be associated with this idea and it is worth distinguishing them and in general penetrating through the metaphor to something more precise. In the third section ("The Sequence of Thoughts"), I consider Geach's criticisms of James's application of the stream view of consciousness to conscious thought. And in the fourth, fifth, and sixth sections, I formulate and assess three different arguments that challenge the view that conscious thoughts have irreducible cognitive phenomenology. Each argument draws on the James/Geach dispute to some extent. In my view they are all inconclusive.

Preliminaries

Aside from the focus on time, the arguments in this chapter are special in three ways. First, they take into account the distinction between mental states and mental events. Second, as already noted, they are concerned with conscious thoughts narrowly construed. Third, they challenge Irreducibility as a thesis about conscious thoughts by supporting a thesis – which I will call Vehicle Proxy – that is incompatible with it. The aim of this section is to sort out some preliminary matters that arise because of these features.

Let us start with the difference between mental states and mental events. We can characterize the difference between them by characterizing the difference between states and events more generally.

As I will understand it, that distinction tracks two different ways of persisting. Consider an event, for example the event of typing a word. If you type from time t_a to time t_b, the typing persists from t_a to t_b in virtue of having temporal parts, or phases, at each of the moments within that interval. In one phase you press the "p" key, in another you press the "r" key, etc. The typing cannot be identified with any of its phases. They are parts of it. Now consider a state, for example sitting. If you sit from time t_a to time t_b, the sitting persists from t_a to t_b in virtue of obtaining at each of the moments within that interval. There need be no phases. There is you and there is the property of sitting and you instantiate the property at t_a and continue to instantiate it till t_b. Your state of sitting can be identified with each of these instantiations; for they are all just the same state continuing to obtain. It is worth noting that the difference between states and events need not be framed in terms of the *having* of temporal parts. One might very well segment a persisting state into temporal parts. The difference is about the grounding of persistence: events persist in virtue of having parts at different times, and states persist in virtue of themselves obtaining at different times.

What we have observed about states and events generally also holds for mental states and mental events specifically. A mental state persists in virtue of obtaining at different times. A mental event persists in virtue of having parts at different times. The distinction between mental states and mental events naturally suggests a distinction between phenomenal states and phenomenal events. Phenomenal states are mental states individuated by what it is like for one to be in them. Phenomenal events are mental events individuated by what it is like for them to occur to one. The distinction between phenomenal states and phenomenal events naturally suggests a distinction between phenomenally conscious states and phenomenally conscious events. Here, however, there is a slight complication.

Instead of defining phenomenally conscious states just in terms of phenomenal states, it will prove useful to define phenomenally conscious states in terms of both phenomenal states and phenomenal events. An analogous point holds for phenomenally conscious events. So the characterizations I will adopt here are these. A mental state M is a phenomenally conscious state just in case necessarily, if one is in M, then because one is in M there is some phenomenal state or event P such that one is in P or P occurs to one. And a mental state M is a phenomenally conscious event just in case necessarily, if M occurs to one, then because M occurs to one there is some phenomenal state or event P such that one is in P or P occurs to one. I am allowing that being in a state might include an event occurring to one and that an event occurring to one might include being in a state. Some of the views I consider below require these possibilities. And they seem like genuine possibilities to me. Being pregnant is a state that includes certain events. And winning a race is an event that includes a certain state.

Now let us consider how we need to modify our understanding of Irreducibility for the purposes of this chapter. As I formulated it in the introduction Irreducibility says: Some cognitive states put one in phenomenal states for which no wholly sensory states suffice. Now we need to take into account phenomenal events and restrict the thesis to conscious thoughts. This suggests the following:

Irreducibility$_{CT}$: Some conscious thoughts make phenomenal differences to one's overall experience for which nothing other than a conscious thought suffices.

The modified form of Irreducibility isolates conscious thoughts from both sensory states and other conscious cognitive states that are not conscious thoughts in the narrow sense under consideration. The idea is that some conscious thoughts have a phenomenal character that cannot be found in either wholly sensory states or events or in other kinds of conscious cognitive states or events.

The arguments in this chapter pose a challenge to Irreducibility$_{CT}$ by supporting a thesis that is incompatible with it. I will adopt the following formulation of the thesis:

Vehicle Proxy: If a conscious thought makes a phenomenal difference to one's overall experience, then it does so just because of the sensory appearance of a vehicle for that thought.

The idea of a vehicle for thought is best illustrated by speech and writing. Take the thought that you have an appointment. You might express this thought in speech or writing by speaking or writing the words, "I have an appointment." The spoken or written words are a vehicle for the thought. In general a vehicle for a thought "carries" that thought's content. According to Vehicle Proxy, if your conscious thought that you have an appointment makes a phenomenal difference to your overall experience, then it does so just because of the sensory appearance of a vehicle expressing the thought that you have an appointment. The vehicle is a phenomenal proxy for the thought – hence the name of the thesis. The vehicle might be inner speech or inner writing or something non-linguistic such as a mental image of the person you have to meet.

If Vehicle Proxy is true, then Irreducibility$_{CT}$ is false. For suppose some conscious thought makes a phenomenal difference to your overall experience. According to Vehicle Proxy it does so just because of the sensory appearance of a vehicle for that thought. There is nothing more to the thought's phenomenal presence than what is accounted for by the sensory appearance of the vehicle. This implies that if you were in some wholly sensory mental state, or if some wholly sensory mental event were to occur to you, representing the same vehicle in the same way, then it would suffice to put you in the same phenomenal state, or make the same phenomenal event occur to you, as does the conscious thought. Hence Irreducibility$_{CT}$ is false.

The stream of consciousness

At different times you have different experiences, but they seem to fit together into one conscious life with an approaching future, a receding past, and a present through which they flow. This suggests the metaphor of the stream of consciousness. If we want to use this idea in arguments, however, we need to make it more precise. That is the aim of this section.

My strategy will be to start with the notion of a minimal stream of consciousness and build up to the notion of a Jamesian stream of consciousness, taking William James as our guide. And I will use a tool from mathematics. Suppose a particle is in motion. At different times it is at different places. We might say that the motion of the particle associates different times with different places. For mathematical purposes it is useful to represent this motion using a function from times to places. The function captures significant structural features of the motion. Now consider a stream of consciousness. At different times it includes different phenomenal states and events. We might say that the stream of consciousness associates different times with different phenomenal states and events. For our purposes it will be useful to represent this stream using a relation from times to phenomenal states and events. The relation will capture significant structural features of the stream of consciousness.

The notion of a minimal stream of consciousness is minimal because all it does is capture the fact that a stream of consciousness associates different times with different phenomenal states and events. There are no additional structural features. So we can define the notion this way: X is a minimal stream of consciousness just in case X is a binary relation between times and instances of phenomenal states or temporal parts of phenomenal events.

Four clarifications are in order. First, as already indicated, strictly speaking the binary relation mentioned in the definition is a mathematical representation of a stream of consciousness, not itself a stream of consciousness. I will follow a common and harmless practice in ignoring this distinction. Second, streams of consciousness consist of tokens not types. The notions of *phenomenal state* and *phenomenal event* are notions of types. Streams of consciousness relate times to instances or temporal parts of instances of these types. Third, the reason for adding the qualification "or temporal parts of" is that some phenomenal events persist, but as pointed out above, they do so by having temporal parts. For a temporally extended phenomenal event to occur to one is for one's stream of consciousness to assign its different temporal parts to the appropriate times. Fourth, streams are not functions from times to instances of phenomenal states or temporal parts of phenomenal events. They are relations between times and instances of phenomenal states or temporal parts of events. Unlike functions, relations can be one-many. This allows a stream to assign more than one token phenomenal state or temporal part of a phenomenal event to the same time. Contrast the motion of a particle: at any one time it is at just one place, so we can use a function to represent that motion.

Now we will build on the minimal notion, following James's discussion in the *Principles of Psychology*. The chapter in which James discusses the stream of consciousness is entitled "The Stream of Thought." In it James defends five claims. Here are his initial formulations of them:

(1)   Every thought tends to be part of a personal consciousness.
(2)   Within each personal consciousness thought is always changing.
(3)   Within each personal consciousness thought is sensibly continuous.
(4)   It always appears to deal with objects independent of itself.
(5)   It is interested in some parts of these objects to the exclusion of others, and welcomes or rejects – *chooses* from among them, in a word – all the while.[2]

For this purpose, the important theses are (1) through (3), and I will organize my discussion around them, setting (4) and (5) aside.

As a preliminary point it is important to observe that James is using "thought" to mean "every form of consciousness indiscriminately."[3] So his theses are about sensory perceptions, bodily sensations, emotions, moods, and various conscious cognitive states. Because this book is about the distinctive properties of cognitive states as opposed to sensory states and this chapter is about the distinctive properties of conscious thoughts narrowly construed as opposed to both sensory states and other cognitive states, I will not use the term "thought" in the way James uses it. Instead of introducing a single alternative term to mean what James meant by "thought" I will continue to use the terms I have already been using – "phenomenal state," "phenomenal event," "phenomenally conscious state," "phenomenally conscious event" – and one other term – "item in a stream of consciousness."

An item in a stream of consciousness is anything that belongs to that stream of consciousness. Mathematical discussions of relations use the notions of domain and range. Relations associate members of the domain to members of the range. For streams of consciousness the domain contains times and the range contains phenomenal states and temporal parts of phenomenal events. So we can say that something is an item in a stream of consciousness just in case it is in the range of the relation representing that stream of consciousness. This is the notion I will use in discussing James. I believe it picks out the same assortment of things he intended to pick out by the term "thought," i.e. "every form of consciousness indiscriminately."

James's first thesis, then, is that every item in a stream of consciousness tends to be part of a personal consciousness. There are two distinct claims James associates with this one thesis.

Common Self: The items in a stream of consciousness belong to a common self.

> Synchronic Unity: The items a stream of consciousness assigns to one time tend to be phenomenally unified.

Your current visual experiences are phenomenally unified with your current auditory experiences. They are not phenomenally unified with mine. Synchronic Unity says that all of your token phenomenal states and events at a time tend to stand in this unifying relation.[4] In this book I will take the notion of synchronic phenomenal unity as basic.[5] James seems to think that Common Self *explains* Synchronic Unity. This is a controversial claim in the current literature.[6] I believe it is easily separated from James's other commitments, so I will not assume it in what follows.

James's second claim is that the items in a stream of consciousness are always changing. In discussing this claim, James distinguishes three theses, to which he takes different attitudes:

> No Endurance: If t_1 and t_2 are different times in the domain of a stream of consciousness, then there is no item of consciousness that the stream assigns to both t_1 and t_2.[7]

> No Recurrence: If t_1, t_2, and t_3 are different times in the domain of a stream of consciousness such that t_2 is between t_1 and t_3, then there is no item of consciousness the stream assigns to t_1 and t_3 but not t_2.[8]

> No Constancy: If t_1 and t_2 are different times in the domain of a stream of consciousness, then there is some item of consciousness the stream assigns to one of t_1 or t_2 but not the other.[9]

James initially considers No Endurance, but remains neutral about it, writing "even if true, that would be hard to establish."[10] He approvingly quotes Mr. Shadworth Hodgson's expression of No Constancy.[11] The bulk of his discussion is dedicated to No Recurrence. His commitment to No Recurrence is part of his rejection of "simple ideas."[12] Though James focuses on No Recurrence, No Constancy seems to me more relevant to articulating the idea that consciousness flows in a stream.

Finally, James's third claim is that streams of consciousness are sensibly continuous. James says that this "means two things:"

> 1. That even where there is a time-gap the consciousness after it feels as if it belonged together with the consciousness before it, as another part of the same self;

2. That the changes from one moment to another in the quality of the consciousness are never absolutely abrupt.[13]

The first subclaim is a temporal analog of Common Self. Here I will set it aside. The second subclaim admits two interpretations. First, it might be about the content of a stream of consciousness, about what is experienced. Second, it might be about the structure of a stream of consciousness, about how its parts are related. James is committed to claims about both. But for our purposes the point about content is irrelevant, so I will set it aside. The point about structure is a temporal analog of Synchronic Unity, and so naturally called Diachronic Unity.

Diachronic Unity: For any time t within the domain of a stream of consciousness, if there is any interval around t, then there is an interval i around t such that the items the stream assigns to t tend to be phenomenally unified with the items the stream assigns to other times within i.[14]

Suppose you are listening to some music. Your present auditory experience of the music is unified with your just past auditory experience of the music. One sign of this is that your present auditory experience of the music is felt as a continued experience of the music, not as an isolated experience of some sounds. Diachronic Unity says that all of your token phenomenal states and events over a certain interval tend to stand in this unifying relation.[15] In this book I will take the notion of diachronic phenomenal unity as basic.[16] I will not try to define it or defend any theory about. In the next section I will take up one point about the relationship between phenomenal unity and mereological notions.

We started out with a minimal notion of a stream of consciousness. According to James actual streams of consciousness possess more properties than those attributed to them in the definition of the minimal notion. In my view the crucial Jamesian features associated with streams of consciousness are those attributed in Synchronic Unity, No Constancy, and Diachronic Unity. So we can define a Jamesian stream of conscious as follows: X is a Jamesian stream of consciousness just in case X is a minimal stream of consciousness for which Synchronic Unity, No Constancy, and Diachronic Unity hold. The claim that actual streams of consciousness are Jamesian streams of consciousness seems to me to constitute a reasonable view of what consciousness is like that does not rely too much on metaphor.

Brian O'Shaughnessy, however, argues that there is more to consciousness being stream-like than the features I have discussed. This is important, not only because of the intrinsic interest of O'Shaughnessy's views on the matter, but also because the arguments I discuss in later sections rely on O'Shaughnessy's augmented understanding of what it is for consciousness to be stream-like.

The aspect of O'Shaughnessy's view that will concern us is his claim that consciousness is processive: "in the realm of experience … whatever endures necessarily does so processively."[17] Before proceeding we need to calibrate terminology. To what notion I have used, if any, does O'Shaughnessy's notion of experience correspond? I believe he is using the notion of experience to pick out portions of a stream of consciousness. The portions are particulars – not types. The portions need not be able to wholly exist at an individual time. So his notion does not correspond to *phenomenal event or state, phenomenally conscious event or state* – which are notions for types. Nor does his notion correspond to *item in a stream of consciousness*, as I have defined that notion, since as I have defined it such items must be able to wholly exist at an individual time. Rather his notion can be understood as follows: X is an experience just in case X is an item or is composed of items in a stream of consciousness. This definition allows experiences to include token phenomenal states and token phenomenal events, not just token phenomenal states and token temporal parts of phenomenal events.

According to O'Shaughnessy, experiences persist like processes. Processes persist like events, not states. It follows that on O'Shaughnessy's view experiences persist like events. That is, any experience that persists for an interval of time does so by having temporal parts at each of the moments within that interval. According to O'Shaughnessy this is part of what makes consciousness stream-like.[18] It is equivalent to the claim that streams of consciousness do not relate times to instances of phenomenal states, just instances of temporal parts of phenomenal events. And this is something that the writers to be considered in the final three sections below accept.

Does O'Shaughnessy's claim that consciousness is processive follow from the fact that consciousness is stream-like in the ways I associated with James? O'Shaughnessy's discussion might give the impression that it does. He gives an argument for the claim that consciousness is processive that rests on the claim that consciousness is in "flux." Here is what he writes:

We have seen that experiences are essentially in a condition of flux. What this means is, that all experiences of necessity "happen" or "occur" or "are going on": in a word, are either events, or processes, or both ... No experiences are states ... Thus, suppose we were to bring mental life to a complete standstill ... Then while many non-experiential states will persist, all non-experiential process would cease and all experiences cease to be (hence the destruction of mental incident entails the destruction of consciousness). Does not this demonstrate that no experiences are states? ... What is an example of a thing endowed with the following pair of properties: being an experience, and such that a cessation of all mental incident need not destroy it?[19]

Here is one way to formulate O'Shaughnessy's line of thought:

(1) The stream of consciousness is essentially in a condition of flux.
(2) So, it is impossible for your stream of consciousness to come to a standstill and for you to have experiences.
(3) If experiences persisted as states, then it would be possible for your stream of consciousness to come to a standstill and for you to have experiences.
(4) So experiences persist as processes, not as states.

The problem with this argument is one pointed out by James. Does O'Shaughnessy's premise (1) correspond to No Endurance or No Constancy?[20] If it corresponds to No Endurance, then there is an understanding of the argument that makes it valid. The idea would be that since no experience persists unchanged, no experience is just the continuation of a state. But, as James pointed out, No Endurance is difficult to establish. There is no direct phenomenological evidence for it. If I stare at an unchanging colored expanse, it seems at least possible that my visual experience of it remains unchanged, even if some of my other experiences must be changing for me to be conscious at all. O'Shaughnessy's view is that even if my visual experience remains unchanged, it remains so by being continually updated. But he cannot assume that this is so, since to do so is to assume that experiences persist processively, which is what needs showing. Suppose, then, O'Shaughnessy's premise (1) corresponds to No Constancy. Then the argument is invalid. Perhaps it is a necessary background condition on streams of consciousness that some of one's experiences change from moment to moment. This is compatible with there also being some enduring, unchanging experiences.

So it is consistent to think that consciousness is stream-like while denying that all experiences persist processively. Insofar as the arguments to be considered below rely on O'Shaughnessy's processive view of experience, then, they have a weak link. I will explore other deficiencies in them, but this is one that should be kept in mind in keeping a tally of the dialectical score.

The sequence of thoughts

Geach's most detailed discussion of his disagreement with James occurs in his essay "What Do We Think With?"[21] There he writes:

> Thinking consists in having a series of thoughts which can be counted off discretely – the first, the second, the third, ... –; which, if complex, must occur with all their elements present simultaneously; which do not pass into one another by gradual transition.[22]

He explicitly contrasts this view with James's: "thoughts occur not in a Jamesian stream, but as I maintain that they do – as a series in which certain thought-contents successively occur; with no succession within any one thought and no gradual transition from one thought to another ... "[23] On the face of it, the relevant dispute between James and Geach can be put rather simply. According to James thoughts flow in a continuous stream. According to Geach thoughts march along in sequential trains. Here, however, we must tread with caution.

Geach makes two claims about the sequential character of thinking. Here are sharper formulations:

> Simultaneity: Suppose you think that p at t. Then all the parts of your thought that p occur at t.

> Disjointness: Suppose you think that p at t_a and think that q at a distinct time t_b. Then there is no overlap between your thought that p and your thought that q – i.e. your thought that p and your thought that q do not share any parts.[24]

Simultaneity is the claim that all the parts of a thought occur simultaneously and Disjointness is the claim that there are no gradual transitions between thoughts.

Neither of these claims is inconsistent with the claim that thoughts flow in a Jamesian stream, as I have characterized such a stream. Simultaneity appears to be inconsistent with James's claim later in the chapter on "The

Stream of Thought," that thoughts have "time-parts."[25] But James's discussion there is rather obscure. He adds:

> Now I say of these time-parts that we cannot take any one of them so short that it will not after some fashion or other be a thought of the whole object ... They melt into each other like dissolving views, and no two of them feel the object just alike, but each feels the total object in a unitary undivided way.[26]

In light of this passage, one might question whether Geach's Simultaneity thesis is really inconsistent with James's claim that thoughts have "time-parts." I set this issue aside, however. Our present concern is with the question of whether Geach's view is inconsistent with the claim that thoughts flow in a Jamesian stream, not with whether Geach's view is inconsistent with any other theses James held about thinking.

To make the separation of these issues clearer, let us consider how Geach's view might be altered so as to generate claims that are clearly inconsistent with the claim that thoughts flow in a Jamesian stream. I will focus on Disjointness, as it is more obviously related to this issue. Here is a first pass:

> Disunity: Suppose you think that p at t_a and think that q at a distinct time t_b. There is no relation of diachronic unity that obtains between your thought that p and your thought that q.

Jamesian streams flow in virtue of relations of diachronic unity, not in virtue of relations of mereological overlap. So to generate an inconsistency we want something like Disunity. But Disunity is not enough. The reason is that James's commitment to Diachronic Unity is about all sorts of items in a stream of consciousness, but Disunity is about thoughts in the narrow sense. Consider the way that the natural numbers occur in the real numbers. They are a discrete subsequence within the richer continuum. Similarly, thoughts might be a discrete subsequence within the richer continuum of experiences in general. If Disunity were true, then there could be no Jamesian stream of consciousness consisting wholly of thoughts, but thoughts could occur within richer streams of consciousness that have their stream-like, flowing character in virtue of diachronic unity relations between items in the stream in general.

It is not clear what motivation there is for holding this view. What bars thoughts from standing in diachronic unity relations to each other? One might argue that diachronic unity relations obtain in virtue of mereological overlap relations. Above I said there is a distinction between diachronic unity and mereological overlap. On the face of it there is. But maybe the right theory of diachronic unity requires two diachronically unified experiences to share parts.[27] This view seems implausible to me, however. A visual experience can be diachronically unified with a gustatory experience, even though they share no parts. Explaining phenomenal unity in mereological terms is an attractive idea, but it is possible to do so without requiring unified experiences to overlap. One idea is that two experiences are unified if they are both parts of a larger experience.[28] They do not need to *share parts*. Rather, they need to *be parts* of a larger experience. This sort of view is compatible with diachronic unity relations holding between non-overlapping thoughts. So Disunity is rather questionable. Still, it is an interesting thesis, worth flagging. It implies that even if thoughts do occur in a stream of consciousness, they could not constitute a stream of consciousness on their own.

To rule out the possibility of thoughts occurring in a Jamesian stream of consciousness at all, we would have to strengthen Disunity to the following:

Discontinuity: Suppose you think that p at t_a and have an experience, e, at a distinct time t_b. There is no relation of diachronic unity that occurs between your thought that p and your experience, e.

If Discontinuity is true, then thoughts introduce disruptions in a stream of consciousness, no matter what other sorts of items that stream contains. This is inconsistent with James's view that the stream of consciousness obeys Diachronic Unity. It is unclear what the motivation for Discontinuity might be.

Let us briefly review. Geach's claim Simultaneity thesis *might* be inconsistent with James's claim that thoughts have time-parts, but this is separate from the issue of whether thoughts occur in a Jamesian stream. Geach's claim Disjointness is also consistent with thoughts occurring in a Jamesian stream. There is an interesting alteration of Disjointness, namely Disunity, that implies that even if thoughts do occur in a Jamesian stream, their doing so depends on the stream containing items other than thoughts. Discontinuity represents a way of ruling out the possibility of thoughts occurring in a Jamesian stream, specifically a stream that obeys Diachronic Unity, but it is unclear what motivation there is for endorsing it.

Finally, let me emphasize that I am not rejecting either of Geach's claims – Simultaneity or Disjointness. Both seem plausible to me. What I am denying is that their truth immediately renders thoughts unsuitable to be parts of a Jamesian stream of consciousness, where such a stream is characterized by Synchronic Unity, No Constancy, and Diachronic Unity.[29]

Thoughts in the stream

The previous two sections reviewed the James/Geach dispute. In this and the next two sections I will consider recent arguments that draw on this dispute in supporting the thesis I have called Vehicle Proxy – that if a conscious thought makes a phenomenal difference to one's overall experience, then it does so just because of the sensory appearance of a vehicle for that thought.

The first argument derives from Soteriou's paper "Content and the Stream of Consciousness."[30]

Soteriou accepts the following two claims:

(1)   All of one's phenomenal states or events are parts of one's stream of consciousness.[31]
(2)   All parts of a stream of consciousness are processive.[32]

Claim (1) seems innocuous in the present context. Claim (2) is equivalent to O'Shaughnessy's claim that experiences are processive.[33]

Together (1) and (2) imply that one is never in phenomenal states – only phenomenal events occur to one. The bulk of Soteriou's paper is dedicated to reconciling (1) and (2) with the existence of phenomenally conscious states, for example the state you are in when it visually seems to you that the sky is blue. In brief, the reconciliation is that phenomenally conscious states exist in *virtue of* the occurrence of phenomenal events.[34] Here Soteriou is exploiting the possibility noted above that one might be in a state in virtue of events occurring to one.

Our concern is with the bearing all this has on conscious thought. Here is a third claim Soteriou accepts:

(3)   Conscious thoughts are not events with duration.[35]

The motivation for (3) comes from Geach's claim that there is no succession within any one thought.[36] Given (1), (2), and (3) we can continue the argument for Vehicle Proxy as follows:

(4) Events that lack duration are not processive. [Premise]

(5) If a conscious thought includes a phenomenal event, then it must include an event that has duration.[37] [From (1), (2), (4)]

(6) If a conscious thought includes an event with duration, then it does so by including an event other than a thought.[38] [From (3)]

(7) So if a conscious thought includes a phenomenal event, then it does so because it includes an event other than a thought – most plausibly a sensible vehicle for the thought. [From (5) and (6)]

The conclusion (7) gives us reason to believe Vehicle Proxy. I will point out two weaknesses in the argument.

The first is premise (2), the premise taken from O'Shaughnessy. Soteriou does not provide independent support for it, and we saw that O'Shaughnessy's own argument in support of it falls short. So the proponent of Irreducibility as applied to conscious thoughts and the opponent of Vehicle Proxy might dig in his or her heels at this point.

The second is premise (4). Recall that something is processive just in case if it persists, then it does so in virtue of having temporal parts. This is compatible with the existence of processive events that lack duration. Perhaps the term "processive" is misleading. It might suggest that the predicate applies to something just in case it persists and it does so by virtue of having temporal parts. But this is a mistake. The idea is that the concept applies to something because of how it would persist if it did persist, and it is neutral about whether that thing does in fact persist.

Of course, one might *stipulate* that "processive" should be applied only to something that persists and does so by having temporal parts. But then it is not clear that O'Shaughnessy's argument, even if it didn't have the problems I pointed out, would establish that all experiences are processive. Nothing about his reflections on the flux of consciousness suggests that experiences must have duration.

Anyway, let us set aside the term "processive." What the foregoing suggests is that thoughts include *instantaneous* phenomenal events. Perhaps they are sometimes phenomenally conscious in part because they include non-instantaneous phenomenal events, such as those associated with sensory vehicles. But perhaps in other cases they are phenomenally conscious just because they include instantaneous phenomenal events, which might themselves be the conscious thoughts. In this case Vehicle Proxy is mistaken.

One might worry: could a phenomenal event be instantaneous? The concept does not seem on its face incoherent to me. Perhaps further consideration will reveal a deep incoherence. If so, this requires additional argumentation. We consider such argumentation in the next section.

Instantaneous thoughts and persisting vehicles

The second argument for Vehicle Proxy also comes from a paper by Soteriou, "Mental Agency, Conscious Thinking, and Phenomenal Character."[39] The argument is that something along the lines of Vehicle Proxy is the best way to solve a certain puzzle about conscious thought.

Here is the puzzle:

(1) What makes a conscious thought conscious is a higher order representation of it.[40]
(2) Conscious thoughts are events.[41]

A consequence Soteriou draws from (1) and (2) is:

(3) If a thought is conscious, then it has duration.[42]

The idea is that either a conscious thought is an instantaneous change in mental state or not. If it is, then "it seems to be the kind of event one can only have access to via one's access to the state that is acquired," and so one can "only conceive of such an event as one that has happened or occurred (or as something that is going to happen), rather than something that is happening."[43] But a conscious thought is felt as something one is doing now, as it occurs. So conscious thoughts are not instantaneous changes in mental state, i.e. given (2), then (3).

But, from Geach again we have:

(4) Thoughts are not events with duration.[44]

The puzzle about conscious thought, then, is that if a thought is conscious it must be an event with duration, but thoughts are not events with duration, so no thought is conscious.

Soteriou does not accept that no thought is conscious. He proposes a solution to the puzzle:

> The solution, I suggest, is to think of the conscious mental act of judging as involving the occurrence of a conscious mental event with duration

that is the vehicle of the mental act of judging, just as, in the case of thinking out loud, the bodily action of one's saying that *p* is the vehicle of one's judging that *p* out loud.[45]

So the proposed solution to the puzzle is Vehicle Proxy. In my view, however, there is no real puzzle. If there is no real puzzle, then this motivation for Vehicle Proxy at least turns out to be spurious.

One weak part of the supposed puzzle is claim (1), that what makes a conscious thought conscious is a higher order representation of it. Some philosophers believe this.[46] But many philosophers deny it. Some deny it because they think that what makes a conscious thought conscious does not involve a representation of it.[47] Others deny it because they think that while what makes a conscious thought conscious does involve a representation of it, the representation is a form of self-representation, not higher order representation.[48]

If one of these alternative views is true, then Soteriou's puzzle does not get off the ground. Suppose what makes a conscious thought conscious does not involve a representation of it. Then it isn't clear how one might reason from the conditions on a thought's being conscious to claim (3) in the puzzle, that if a thought is conscious, then it has duration. Further, suppose that what makes a conscious thought conscious involves a form of self-representation. Then the bit of reasoning Soteriou develops from the conditions on a thought's being conscious to claim (3) does not seem persuasive. That reasoning, recall, depended on the idea that a representation of an instantaneous event cannot represent it as occurring now. But if the representation is itself identical to or a part of the instantaneous event, as self-representationalist views suggest, then it is unclear why this should be so. It is not as if the thought is too quick for the representation – since the representation is just as quick as the thought. So really, at most, Soteriou's apparent puzzle is a genuine puzzle only given a controversial higher order view about what makes a conscious thought conscious.

Even granting such a higher order view, however, Soteriou's puzzle can be resisted. The reasoning in Soteriou's puzzle is from (1) that what makes a conscious thought conscious is a higher order representation and (2) that conscious thoughts are events, to (3) that if a thought is conscious, then it has duration; and then given (4) that thoughts are not events with duration, to the conclusion that there are no conscious thoughts. But the following reasoning seems just as plausible to me. From (1), (2), and (4) conclude that if a thought is conscious, then the higher order representation in virtue of which it is conscious is instantaneous. I find both bits of reasoning somewhat less than transparent, since it is doubtful that the temporal properties of an event constrain the temporal properties of representations of that event.[49] The point I want to emphasize for now is just that Soteriou's reasoning is not obviously better than the alternative. But the alternative does not lead to any puzzling conclusion about the non-existence of conscious thoughts.

So there are reasons for thinking the apparent puzzle motivating Vehicle Proxy is not really a puzzle.

Persisting thoughts and persisting vehicles

The third and final argument for Vehicle Proxy that I will consider occurs in Tye and Wright's paper "Is There a Phenomenology of Thought?"[50]

The first premise in the argument comes from O'Shaughnessy. It is O'Shaughnessy's claim that experiences persist like processes, not like states:

(1)   Experiences, i.e. parts of the stream of consciousness, persist by having temporal parts.[51]

The second premise is motivated by reflection on Geach's work. Unlike Soteriou, however, Tye and Wright do not defend a claim that calls into question the duration of conscious thoughts. This is because they do not argue that conscious thoughts are events. What they take from Geach is a premise about how thoughts persist, if they do at all:

(2)   If a thought persists, it does not do so by having temporal parts, but rather by enduring, like a state.[52]

Next, they observe that some phenomenally conscious thoughts do persist, and, given (1), do so processively:

(3)   Some phenomenally conscious thoughts persist, and do so processively.[53]

Notice that though (2) and (3) are in tension, (2) is about thoughts, and (3) is about phenomenally conscious thoughts. There are ways to exploit this difference to relieve the tension.[54] This is the move Tye and Wright suggest. According to them if a phenomenally conscious thought persists it does so by virtue of a sensory vehicle persisting:

(4)   If a phenomenally conscious thought persists, it does so because it is associated with a sensory vehicle that persists.[55]

If (4) is true, it lends some support to a more general conclusion:

(5)   If a thought is phenomenally conscious – i.e. puts one in a phenomenal state or event – it is phenomenally conscious because it is associated with a phenomenally conscious sensory vehicle.[56]

The conclusion (5) is just a variant on Vehicle Proxy.

As with the arguments from the previous two sections, a weak point in this argument is its reliance on the under-supported premise from O'Shaughnessy that experiences persist processively. So the opponent of Vehicle Proxy might resist the argument's first premise.

My main worry with the argument has to do with (2) and (3). Soteriou, reflecting on the same passages from Geach, did not draw a conclusion like (2). Rather he concluded that thoughts are events without duration. If there is motivation for resisting this line of reasoning and preferring Tye and Wright's (2) it must be whatever is also motivating (3). But (3), it seems to me, introduces a new kind of mental state or event.

It is one thing to simply think that p, say that you have an appointment or that any number not on some supposed finite list of primes must be composite and so divisible by some number on the list. It is another thing to hold the thought that p in mind. Suppose I am working out the proof that there are an infinite number of primes. I have my supposed list of primes. The thought that any number not on it must be composite and so divisible by some number on the list occurs to me. This is simply thinking that p. But suppose I don't know how to proceed in the proof. So I hold the thought that any number not on the list must be composite and so divisible by some number on the list in mind, as I try to figure out how to go on. This is not *simply* thinking that p. It is not as if in holding the thought in mind I just prolong whatever it was that happened when the thought that any number not on it must be composite and so divisible by some number on the list occurred to me. Rather, holding this thought in mind will partly consist in other mental states and events obtaining or occurring. For example, various other thoughts about how I might use this proposition in proceeding with the proof will occur to me. Holding the thought that p in mind is not merely bearing a certain attitude – judging, entertaining, recollecting, or whatever – to the proposition that p. It is a more complicated mental state or event that consists in various other mental states or events obtaining or occurring. Holding the thought that p in mind is cognitive. And it can be counted as having a propositional attitude structure: there is the holding-in-mind attitude and there is the proposition that p. But it does not *just* have a propositional attitude structure. It is more like reasoning through a proof – and in fact is often involved in reasoning through a proof. The significance of this is that claims about the temporal profile of states or events such as thinking that p need not be true of states or events such as holding the thought that p in mind, and vice versa.

So the argument equivocates. Suppose we focus on thinking that p. Then *maybe* (2) is true, but one might resist it and argue instead that thoughts are events without duration. Either way (3) is not true. Merely thinking that p probably does not persist, and certainly does not persist like an event, for exactly the reasons Geach and Soteriou emphasize. Suppose we focus on holding the thought that p in mind. Then, *maybe* (3) is true. Surely holding the thought that p in mind is a state or event that can persist. What is less clear is that it has to be an event. One might argue that it is an event. But then (2) will fail. (2) will only seem plausible if we equivocate and refocus on simply thinking that p, not holding the thought that p in mind. On the other hand, one might argue that holding the thought that p in mind is really a state. In this case (2) will remain true. Part of (3) will be true – the part about persistence. But part will be false – the part about persistence as an event. One might worry in this case about the impact of premise (1), supposing we concede it for now. But there is really no problem. For holding the thought that p in mind might be a phenomenally conscious state that one is in because various phenomenal events occur to one. Further, these phenomenal events need not involve vehicles. They can just be conscious thought events – thinkings that p – that themselves lack duration. In this case one holds the thought that p in mind by having various thoughts, some might be thoughts that p, but some might be thoughts related to p, e.g. thoughts about how to use the proposition that any number not on a supposed list of all the primes must be composite and so divisible by some number on the list in the proof. I emphasize that I am just pointing out options here. The fact that these are options shows that Tye and Wright's argument for Vehicle Proxy fails.

Notes

1 The proposition that $2 + 2 = 4$ and the proposition that bachelors are unmarried are both true relative to all the ways the world could be. But, on the face of it, they are different propositions. One way to draw the distinction is to consider both ways the world could be – possible worlds – and ways the world could not be – impossible worlds. So we might say that propositions are true or false both relative to different ways the world could be and relative to different ways the world could not be. The propositions that $2 + 2 = 4$ and that bachelors are unmarried are distinct because they are true relative to different ways the world could not be. See Jago 2014 for a view along these lines.

2 James 1983, 220.

3 Ibid., 219–220.

4 I'm following James in hedging the claim so that it is about a tendency not a necessity. Nothing will hinge on the difference.

5 For helpful discussion see Dainton 2000/2006, Bayne and Chalmers 2003, Tye 2003, and Bayne 2010.

6 See Dainton 2000/2006 for a challenge to it.

7 See "no one state of mind has any duration" and surrounding discussion (James 1983, 224).

8 See "no state once gone can recur and be identical with what it was before" and surrounding discussion (ibid.).

9 See "we all recognize as different great classes of our conscious states" and surrounding discussion (ibid.).

10 Ibid.

11 Ibid., 224–225.

12 Ibid., 225–230.

13 Ibid., 231.

14 The condition "if there is any interval around t" is meant to set aside cases in which one just comes to consciousness or cases in which one is just about to fall into unconsciousness. James discusses these cases as well, but they are irrelevant to my present concerns.

15 Just as with Synchronic Unity I am following James in hedging the claim so that it is about a tendency not a necessity. Again nothing will hinge on the difference.

16 For helpful discussion see, again, Dainton 2000/2006, Bayne and Chalmers 2003, Tye 2003, and Bayne 2010.

17 O'Shaughnessy 2000, 44.

18 Ibid., 43.

19 Ibid., 47.

20 No Recurrence seems irrelevant.

21 In Geach 1969.

22 Ibid., 35.

23 Ibid., 35–36.

24 To be plausible the claim must be about thought tokens and their parts, not thought types and their parts.

25 James 1983, 269.

26 Ibid.

27 See Dainton 2000/2006 for a view of this sort.

28 See Bayne and Chalmers 2003 and Bayne 2010 for this sort of view.

29 This section does raise the question: what exactly did Geach take to constitute a Jamesian stream of consciousness? This is a question of scholarship that I will not pursue here. The obscure "time-parts" passage will likely play an important role in any such investigation.

30 Soteriou 2007. Soteriou does not present himself as a critic of irreducible cognitive phenomenology. There is, however, a line of thought in his paper that does seem to challenge it – at least in the case of conscious thoughts narrowly construed – by supporting a thesis like Vehicle Proxy. See Bayne and Montague 2011, 26, and Tye and Wright 2011, 341ff. Soteriou presents the same line of argument in his book (Soteriou 2013), but I will draw on the earlier work since the discussion there is more focused.

31 Soteriou 2007, 550: "What is distinctive of these phenomenally conscious aspects of mind is the fact that they have an ontological profile that makes them suited to feature in the stream of consciousness."

32 Ibid., 548: "Implicit in the metaphor of the stream of consciousness is the idea that aspects of mind that make up the stream must unfold over time in a way that mental states, like belief, do not."

33 See ibid., 547ff.

34 Ibid., 558: "The phenomenally conscious mental states are those whose obtaining requites the occurrence of phenomenally conscious mental events, or processes."

35 Ibid., 547: "All of this points to the conclusion that 'judge that p' is an achievement, and a plausible account of what it is that an achievement picks out is that it is used to mark an instantaneous event that is some kind of change of state. Hence the conclusion that the mental act of judging lacks duration."

36 See ibid., 544ff.

37 See especially ibid., 562.

38 See ibid., 560–562.

39 Soteriou 2009. The observations about Soteriou (2007) apply here as well. That is, though Soteriou does not present himself as a critic of irreducible cognitive phenomenology, there is a line of thought in his paper that does seem to raise a challenge for it in the case of conscious thoughts. And though Soteriou presents the same line of argument in his book (Soteriou 2013), I will draw on the earlier work since the discussion there is more focused.

40 Soteriou 2009, 238: "This may suggest that we should go for some sort of higher order account of what it is for the mental episodes or acts that constitute one's conscious thinking to be conscious." This is a suggestion Soteriou takes and assumes for the rest of his paper.

41 Ibid., 238: "If we are to accommodate the idea that an agent can apparently be doing something when consciously thinking, then it seems that the objects of the higher order states must include events, and not just other mental states." Soteriou also invokes O'Shaughnessy in motivating (2).

42 Soteriou 2009, 239: "This might suggest that in the case of a conscious mental act the object of the higher order state must be a mental event with duration, and not a mental event that is the mere acquisition of a state with content and nothing more."

43 Ibid., 238.

44 Ibid., 241: "If we take the mental act of judging that p as an example of the kind of mental event involved in conscious thinking, then it does not seem to be the kind of event that *can* unfold in time. It is not the kind of mental event that has duration."

45 Ibid., 242.

46 See, for example, Armstrong 1968, Lycan 1996, Rosenthal 1986.

47 See, for example, Dretske 1993, Chalmers 1996, Siewert 1998.

48 See, for example, Kriegel 2009, Thomasson 2000, and the papers collected in Part 1 of Kriegel and Williford 2006.

49 See Dennett and Kinsbourne 1992.

50 Tye and Wright 2011.

51 See ibid., 341–342.

52 Ibid., 342: "In the language of persistence, thoughts endure (they are wholly present at each moment that they exist), but, unlike processes, they do not perdure (or exist over time in virtue of having distinct parts at each moment of existence)."

53 Ibid., 342: "And yet, one can think that claret is delightful for some time, and the experience of thinking that claret is delightful can seem to unfold before one's mind in a processive fashion."

54 This move depends on not equating "X is a phenomenally conscious thought" with "X is a thought and X is phenomenally conscious." Compare: "X is a fake duck" is not the same as "X is a duck and X is fake." The exact alternative understanding of "X is a phenomenally conscious thought" that one adopts will depend on one's theory. For an example see note 56.

55 Tye and Wright 2011, 342: "What is it that unfolds over time if not the thought? One obvious suggestion is that it is that which accompanies the thought ... as we've seen, such things include the unfolding of linguistic, phonological, and orthographic images, as well as the mental imagery that might accompany one's thinking the thought."

56 Tye and Wright do not highlight the generalization from persisting phenomenally conscious thoughts to all phenomenally conscious thoughts, but it is clear from their discussion that they accept it. (5) gives us the sort of theory mentioned in note 54. According to the theory, "X is a phenomenally conscious thought" will amount to "X is a thought and X is associated with a sensory vehicle that is phenomenally conscious." One might worry that this account implies that even Phenomenal Presence is false.

Further reading

James discusses the "stream of thought" in James (1983). Geach criticizes James in Geach (1969). Arguments bearing on cognitive phenomenology that draw on Geach's criticisms of James occur in Soteriou (2007, 2009, 2013) and Tye and Wright (2011). Dainton (2000/2006), Bayne and Chalmers (2003), Tye (2003), and Bayne (2010) are useful starting points for thinking about the unity of consciousness.

5

INDEPENDENCE

Independence, recall, is the thesis that some cognitive states put one in phenomenal states that are independent of – i.e. that neither necessarily include nor necessarily exclude – sensory states. So far we have noted two things about Independence.

First, in the introduction, I pointed out that Irreducibility does not logically imply Independence. Suppose P is an irreducibly cognitive phenomenal state. It follows that no wholly sensory state suffices for it. But it does not follow that any wholly cognitive state suffices for it. P might be essentially cognitive and essentially sensory. In that case P would be a phenomenal state for which Irreducibility but not Independence holds.

Second, in chapter 2, I pointed out that Independence is at least questionable. If Independence is true, then there could be cognitive phenomenal states in the absence of any sensory phenomenal states. Kriegel's Zoe argument purported to establish the existence of such purely cognitive phenomenal states. But we saw that this argument relies on a questionable premise about a phenomenal contrast that is merely postulated in a hypothetical pair of cases rather than observed for oneself in a pair of cases drawn from one's own experience.

The aim of this chapter is to examine reasons for thinking that though Irreducibility does not logically imply Independence, the questionability of Independence infects Irreducibility nonetheless. I distinguish two different argumentative strategies. Jesse Prinz pursues the first. I call it the extra modality argument. The basic idea is that just as sensory modalities are independent of each other, if there are cognitive phenomenal states, then they form a cognitive modality that should be independent of the sensory modalities. Adam Pautz suggests the second strategy. I call it the missing explanation argument. The basic idea is that absent a special reason to think otherwise, distinct phenomenal states should be assumed independent.

Here is the plan. In the first section, I present Prinz's extra modality argument. In the second ("Interdependence of Sensory and Cognitive States"), I give some reasons to doubt that if there are cognitive phenomenal states, then they form an independent cognitive modality. In the third, I present the missing explanation argument suggested by Pautz's work. In the fourth section ("Phenomenal Holism"), I consider a potential explanation why in general cognitive phenomenal states are not independent of sensory phenomenal states.

The extra modality argument

Jesse Prinz gives the following argument against the existence of cognitive phenomenal states − what he calls "distinctively cognitive phenomenal qualities":

> Shapes, sounds, and smells can all be recombined, and, when conditions are right, experienced without other conscious qualities, as under conditions of intense focal attention. If there were distinctively cognitive phenomenal qualities, then there is no reason to suppose that they are no different in this respect. We should be able to experience them in isolation ... [But] I have encountered no compelling example of an imageless, dispassionate, languageless, conscious thought. If there were cognitive phenomenology, examples should be abundant, just as we can readily bring before the mind an endless range of contours and melodies.[1]

One worry about Prinz's argument is that it does not clearly distinguish between combinations of objects of phenomenal states (shapes, sounds, and smells) and combinations of phenomenal states themselves − visual, auditory, and olfactory appearances. Prinz's intention, however, is clear. Phenomenal states in different sensory modalities are independent of each other. If there are cognitive phenomenal states then they form a category that is relevantly like a sensory modality. So if Irreducibility is true, then Independence is true. But from what we can observe and imagine, there is reason to doubt Independence. So there is reason to doubt Irreducibility.

One might worry about the claim that phenomenal states in different sensory modalities are independent of each other. Sure, there are people who can hear but not see and people who can see but not hear. But maybe the auditory phenomenal states of those who hear but do not see are subtly different from the auditory phenomenal states of those who both hear and see. Similarly, maybe the visual phenomenal states of those who see but do not hear are subtly different from the visual phenomenal states of those who both see and hear. In a classic study, Harry McGurk and John MacDonald showed that what one sees can influence what one hears.[2] For example, if you see someone move their lips to form the syllable /ga-ga/ while the syllable /ba-ba/ is sounded, then you will hear the syllable /da-da/.

Plausibly this influence is merely causal, however. Visual and auditory processes jointly cause you to be in one auditory phenomenal state rather than another. But this does not show that one could not get in that same auditory phenomenal state in a way that does not depend on being in any visual phenomenal states. You might just hear /da-da/. Absent further considerations, Prinz's claim that sensory modalities are independent seems on its face compelling.

In the next section I consider the claim that if there are cognitive phenomenal states, then they form a category that is relevantly like an extra sensory modality.

Interdependence of sensory and cognitive states

Let us suppose Irreducibility is true and there are cognitive phenomenal states. The aim of this section is to explore what dependence relations might hold between these states and sensory states. I will sketch some reasons for thinking that typical cognitive phenomenal states depend on sensory states and that sensory states that occur in the context of phenomenally conscious cognition depend on cognitive phenomenal states. If these reasons are cogent, then we should reject the claim that the cognitive phenomenal states we are supposing to exist must form a category that is relevantly like an extra sensory modality. And this undermines the extra modality argument.

Consider some typical cognitive phenomenal states. Here are some examples:

- The phenomenal state associated with understanding some bit of speech
- The phenomenal state associated with grasping a geometrical proof that uses a diagram
- The phenomenal state associated with intuiting a geometrical truth by visualizing a shape.

These cognitive phenomenal states are also essentially partly sensory phenomenal states. Understanding speech requires sensory presentation of the speech. Grasping a proof that uses a diagram requires sensory presentation of the diagram. And intuiting a truth by visualizing a shape requires sensory presentation of the shape. Once one considers the examples it is just obvious that typical cognitive phenomenal states depend on sensory states. Recognizing this does not undermine the idea that these states are irreducibly cognitive. But it does undermine the idea that these states are purely cognitive and independent of sensory states.

One might reply in two ways.

First, one might argue that the examples of understanding, grasping, and intuiting factor into two separable components. There is the sensory component. And there is an associated cognitive component. The compound state is obviously partly sensory. But this is just because it is a compound state, not because the cognitive part of it is essentially tied to the sensory part of it.

Second, one might concede that some cognitive phenomenal states are also essentially sensory, but argue that if Irreducibility is true, then there should also be purely cognitive phenomenal states that might occur in the absence of any sensory states. Even if the whole class of cognitive phenomenal states fails to form a category that is like an extra sensory modality, perhaps some special subclass of cognitive phenomenal states forms such a category. It is the implied possibility but non-actuality and unimaginability of isolated members in this special subclass that one might think gives strength to Prinz's argument.

Both replies attribute more commitments to proponents of Irreducibility than what logically follows from Irreducibility. In order to be convincing, then, they should be supplemented with considerations that make clear why anyone should add these extra commitments to Irreducibility.

The first reply seems to me to run into a problem here. Naive reflection on the examples of understanding, grasping, and intuiting does not suggest that these are compound states that factor into separable sensory and cognitive components. So if we are to analyze them in this way, then we need some special reason to do so. The first reply does not immediately suggest such a reason. So it is at least incomplete.

The second reply is on more solid ground. Consider conscious cognitive states with the structure of a propositional attitude – conscious thoughts in the narrow sense isolated in the previous chapter (pp. 79–80). These include judging, supposing, entertaining, and recollecting. Unlike the examples of understanding, grasping, and intuiting the example conscious thoughts in the narrow sense do not clearly involve being in any sensory states. So if there is a connection to sensory states it is a non-obvious one. Perhaps further reflection will turn up such a connection. I will return to this issue below. For now I would like to point out that even if the idea that conscious thoughts in the narrow sense have irreducibly cognitive phenomenal characters proves to be problematic on the sorts of grounds Prinz gives, that does not undermine Irreducibility, since there remains the broader class of conscious cognitive states.

Now let us consider dependence in the other direction: are there sensory states that depend on cognitive states? In the balance of this section I will consider reasons for thinking the answer is yes. Some sensory states depend on cognitive states of which they are parts. These are cases of a part depending on a whole to which it belongs. The idea is familiar from work by gestalt psychologists. Gestalt theoretical ideas will play an important role in the fourth section ("Phenomenal Holism") as well, and it will be useful to introduce some of the relevant machinery here.

Consider Wertheimer's famous summary of what gestalt psychology is all about:

> The fundamental "formula" of Gestalt theory might be expressed this way: There are wholes, the behavior of which is not determined by that of their individual elements, but where the part-processes are themselves determined by the intrinsic nature of the whole.[3]

Wertheimer makes two claims. The first is negative: there are mental states (wholes) certain properties of which are not explained by their composition out of certain other mental states (parts) that have certain properties. The second is positive: there are mental states (parts) certain properties of which are explained by the role they play in composing other mental states (wholes) that have certain properties. These claims could use further elaboration: the negative claim is trivial if there are mental states that lack parts; the positive claim is trivial if among the "certain properties" of parts is the property of being a part of a whole. The gestalt psychologists did not bother about formulating principles immune to such worries. Their main agenda was to develop psychological explanations. And Wertheimer's aim in the quoted passage was to highlight a certain feature of the kinds of explanations they pursued: the explanations are what we might call *downward* psychological explanations – they explain the properties of parts by the properties of the wholes those parts compose.

To fix ideas, here is an example.[4] Look at figures A and B:

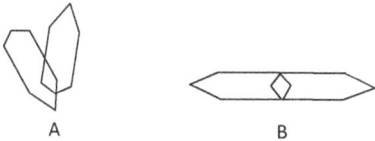

A   B

Here are two facts about the visual experiences subjects typically have in looking at these figures:

- In A, the diamond looks like an area where two hexagons overlap – not like a figure inscribed in an eleven-sided polygon.
- In B, the diamond looks like a figure inscribed in a single hexagon – not like an area where two hexagons overlap.

On reflection and further examination, one might very well see the diamond in A as a figure inscribed in an eleven-sided polygon, and the diamond in B as an area where two hexagons overlap. But this is not what typically happens. Why? The explanation that Wertheimer suggests invokes the Law of Prägnanz – that "psychological organization will always be as 'good' as the prevailing conditions allow," where "the term 'good' is undefined," but "embraces such properties as regularity, symmetry, simplicity ... "[5] Here is a sketch of how one might appeal to this law in explaining the typical responses to figures A and B: two overlapping hexagons are simpler than one eleven-sided polygon, and so by the Law of Prägnanz that is how our visual state organizes the stimuli in A; one hexagon is simpler than two, and so by the law of Prägnanz that is how our visual state organizes the stimuli in B. Set aside the question of whether this is a good explanation, and whether the Law of Prägnanz is a genuine psychological law. The point of the example is to illustrate the sort of downward psychological explanation that the gestalt psychologists favored: a property of the whole (greater simplicity in organization) explains a property of the part – the way the diamond looks.

Gestalt psychology is concerned with giving psychological explanations. These explanations need not reveal the essential properties of phenomenal states. But gestalt theoretical ideas can be invoked in another way, precisely in order to address questions about the essential properties of phenomenal states. We might call this project gestalt phenomenology to distinguish it from gestalt psychology.

Psychologists such as Wertheimer, Koffka, and Köhler endorsed gestalt phenomenology in addition to gestalt psychology. But the philosopher Aron Gurwitsch did the most to promote gestalt phenomenology. Here is a passage in which he discusses its principal tenet:

> [(a)] It is the functional significance of any part of a Gestalt-contexture that makes this part that which it is. The part is what it is only as a constituent of the Gestalt-contexture and as integrated into its unity. Any part of a Gestalt may then be said to be determined as to its existence by its functional significance in the sense that the part only exists in, and is defined by, its functional significance. [(b)] Properties and characters which qualify any constituent of a Gestalt as that which it is in a concrete case, belong to it on account of its functional significance, and of its integration into the Gestalt-contexture. Such determinations belong to the part in question only insofar, and as long, as it is thus integrated.[6]

I've split the passage into two parts, (a) and (b). In part (a) Gurwitsch says that there are some partial phenomenal states that are metaphysically dependent on – that can only exist in – whole phenomenal states; gestalts are structured whole phenomenal states that have such metaphysically dependent parts. In part (b) Gurwitsch says that there are some "characters," i.e. phenomenal characters, that can qualify a phenomenal state only insofar as it is part of a certain whole.

Parts (a) and (b) fit together given that phenomenal states have their phenomenal characters essentially. We have been making this assumption, and Gurwitsch seems to embrace it as well. On the other hand, he – and other proponents of gestalt phenomenology – do sometimes speak as if there are partial phenomenal states that feel one way in one whole phenomenal state and would have felt another way in another whole phenomenal state. Return, for example, to the visual states we are typically in when looking at figures A and B – call them state A and state B. Suppose state A actually occurs and state B might have occurred, and focus on the diamond-presenting part of state A. Consider three different claims about this part:

(1)   It could have been part of B.
(2)   If it were part of B, it would have had a different phenomenal character.
(3)   It has its phenomenal character essentially.

These three claims are mutually inconsistent. I will assume that (3) is non-negotiable. (2) is plausible: were the diamond-presenting part a part of state B it would have represented the diamond as an inscribed figure, not a region of overlap. So the claim that should be given up is (1). It is not the case that there is a partial phenomenal state that while actually a part of state A, could have been a part of state B. The most we should say is: had state B occurred, it would have had a diamond-presenting part, and this part would have been phenomenally similar to the diamond-presenting part of state A.

Let us formulate the main thesis of gestalt phenomenology this way:

Gestaltism: Some partial phenomenal states depend on whole phenomenal states to which they belong.

Consider again the phenomenal states A and B discussed above. The diamond-presenting part of A represents the diamond as a region of overlap. The diamond-presenting part of B represents the diamond as an inscribed figure. These are phenomenal differences. So the two diamond-presenting parts are different phenomenal states. According to Gestaltists, the diamond-presenting partial phenomenal states can only occur as parts that play distinctive roles in composing certain whole visual phenomenal states. What reason is there for making this additional claim? The main reason is that it is impossible to imagine a visual phenomenal state that is qualified just like the diamond-presenting part of A, or the diamond-presenting part of B, without also being part of a whole phenomenal state that is at least largely similar to A, or a whole phenomenal state that is at least largely similar to B. The idea is that we should take the impossibility of imagining such partial phenomenal states as evidence that there can be no such partial phenomenal states. Hence Gestaltism.

Consider some other examples. Compare the following figures:

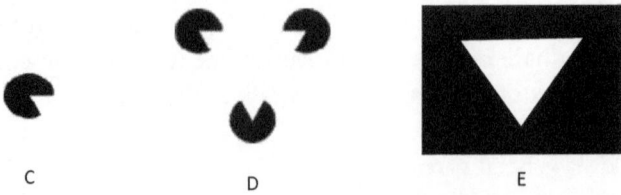

C   D   E

Compare the way the pie in figure C looks with the way the upper left pie in figure D looks. In figure C the pie looks like a pie with a wedge cut out. In figure D the pie looks like a pie that is partially occluded by a triangle. Now compare the triangle in figure D with the triangle in figure E. The triangle in figure D looks like it hovers above three pies. The triangle in figure E looks like it is cut out of a black patch. The differences I have pointed out are phenomenal differences. Further, they seem to derive from the role the respective partial phenomenal states play in composing the whole phenomenal states to which they belong. Let us just focus on figure D. According to Gestaltists, the upper-left-pie-presenting part of our visual presentation of figure D has a phenomenal character that only partial visual states that play similar roles in similar whole visual states can have. The main reason for endorsing the Gestaltist view, again, is the impossibility of imagining visual states having the same phenomenal characters by themselves or as parts of very different whole visual states.

Consider the visual phenomenal states associated with looking at the following two figures:

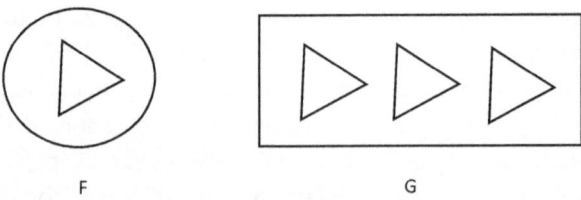

F   G

The triangle in F might appear to point in any of three directions. The leftmost triangle in G also might appear to point in any of three directions, but there is a tendency for it to appear to point along the axis of symmetry of the whole of figure G. Consider two visual states: an F-state representing the triangle in F as pointing rightward, and a G-state representing the leftmost triangle in G as pointing along the axis of symmetry of the whole of figure G – that is, rightward. It is natural to say of this G-state that the axis of symmetry determined by the whole of figure G contributes to making the leftmost triangle in G appear to point rightward. This suggests that the whole visual state is a gestalt.

There is a similarity between the F-state and the G-state. Focus on the triangle-presenting part of the F-state and the leftmost triangle-presenting part of our G-state. Both partial phenomenal states present an equilateral triangle pointing rightward. The partial F-state and the partial G-state are nonetheless different phenomenal states. Why? Plausibly because of the way each partial phenomenal state presents the orientation of the triangle. Consider the property of pointing rightward. Both our partial phenomenal states present that property. But they do so differently. Plausibly this derives from the fact that they use different frames of reference. The partial F-state presents the property of pointing rightward as the property of pointing 3 o'clock on the circle, and the partial G-state presents the property of pointing rightward as the property of pointing along the axis of symmetry of the whole of figure G.[7] Three o'clock is no more distinguished than 7 o'clock or 11 o'clock. Plausibly, that is part of the reason the F-state representing the triangle as pointing 3 o'clock is no more likely to occur than the alternative F-state representing the triangle as pointing 7 o'clock or 11 o'clock. The axis of symmetry of G is, however, a distinguished feature of figure G. Plausibly, that is part of the reason the G-state representing the leftmost triangle as pointing along the axis of symmetry of G is more likely to occur than the alternative G-state representing the leftmost triangle as pointing in its other possible directions. This way of thinking about the partial phenomenal states shows how their phenomenal characters are bound up with the larger phenomenal states within which they occur.

The gestalt phenomenal state associated with looking at figure D and the gestalt phenomenal state associated with looking at figure G illustrate what Gurwitsch calls different "gestalt connections."[8] The difference will matter later, and is worth exploring a bit further.

Consider Rubin's Vase:

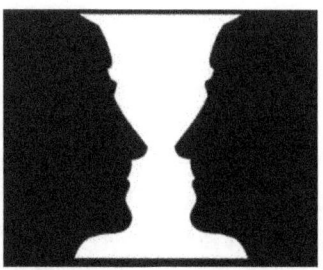

The physical image that constitutes Rubin's Vase gives rise to two different whole phenomenal states. Both phenomenal states have two parts: one part represents something as figure and the other part represents something as ground. The phenomenal states differ, however, in what is represented as figure and what is represented as ground. In one, the figure part of your phenomenal state represents two black faces and the ground part of your phenomenal state represents a white expanse. In the other, the figure part of your phenomenal state represents one white vase and the ground part of your phenomenal state represents a black expanse. There is reason to think that both phenomenal states are gestalts. Take, for example, the phenomenal state in which a vase appears as figure. The figure part of this phenomenal state depends for its phenomenal character on its occurring within a whole phenomenal state that includes the ground part.[9]

This phenomenal state, however, is more like the phenomenal state associated with looking at figure G than it is like the phenomenal state associated with looking at figure D. The reason is that just as you could represent the same orientation in a different frame of reference, you could represent the same type of vase against a different background.

Here is how Gurwitsch puts it in his book, The Field of Consciousness:

> Rubin's figures are independent of the ground, in that their actual location appears as contingent and extrinsic. Every such figure appears as displaceable on the ground from which it actually emerges and also as transferable from one ground to another (in the case of a black figure from a white ground to a red one), without any impairment of its phenomenal identity.[10]

This can seem puzzling. How can it be true that (a) the figure phenomenal state representing a white vase can be recombined with different ground phenomenal states representing different backgrounds "without any impairment of its phenomenal identity," and (b) the whole phenomenal state of which the figure phenomenal state is a part is a gestalt? The answer is that by "phenomenal identity" Gurwitsch does not mean entire phenomenal character. He means something different, a partial determinant of phenomenal character.

Let us distinguish between two aspects of phenomenal character.[11] I'll call the first aspect *phenomenally conscious content*. This is the property of presenting certain things and properties. The phenomenal state associated with looking at figure C and the partial phenomenal state presenting the upper left pie in figure D are phenomenally different because of a difference in phenomenally conscious content: one presents the pie as missing a wedge, and one presents the pie as occluded by a triangle. I'll call the second aspect *phenomenally conscious manner*. This is the property of presenting certain things and properties in a certain manner. The phenomenal state associated with looking at figure F and seeing the triangle as pointing rightward and the partial phenomenal state presenting the leftmost triangle in figure G as pointing rightward are phenomenally different because of a difference in phenomenally conscious manner: both present the property of pointing rightward, but they do so differently.

The phenomenal character of a phenomenal state includes both sorts of phenomenal property. What Gurwitsch has in mind when he talks about "phenomenal identity" is the phenomenally conscious content of a phenomenal state, not the entire phenomenal character of a phenomenal state, which includes both its phenomenally conscious content and the phenomenally conscious manner in which that phenomenally conscious content is presented.[12] So Gurwitsch's point about the Rubin Vase can be put like this. Two figure phenomenal states representing a white vase combined with different ground phenomenal states representing different backgrounds can have the same phenomenally conscious content. But the whole phenomenal states of which the figure phenomenal states are parts are still gestalts because the figure phenomenal states depend for their exact phenomenally conscious manners on the whole phenomenal states of which they are parts. The idea is that the figure phenomenal states representing a white vase represent a white vase in a distinctive manner, fixed by the distinctive background against which the vase stands in relief.[13] The background is like a frame of reference.

Now we can say what the two types of gestalt connection Gurwitsch distinguishes are. In one type a partial phenomenal state depends on the whole phenomenal state of which it is a part for its phenomenally conscious *content*. In the other type a partial phenomenal state depends on the whole phenomenal state of which it is a part for its phenomenally conscious *manner*. In both types a partial phenomenal state depends on the whole phenomenal state of which it is a part – the difference is in the nature of the dependence.

So far we've just considered sensory wholes and their sensory parts. Now let us consider a cognitive whole with sensory parts.

Consider, then, the following proof that the sum of the first n positive integers is half of $n \times (n + 1)$.

Proof: The first n positive integers can be represented by a triangular array of dots, as in the first diagram:

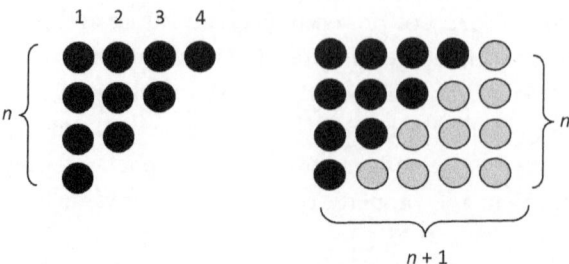

Two of these triangular arrays can be fit together to form a rectangular array containing $n \times (n + 1)$ dots, as in the second diagram. Each triangular array is half of the rectangular array. So, the sum of the first n positive integers is half of $n \times (n + 1)$.

Grasping this proof is a phenomenally conscious cognitive state. Part of this cognitive state is a certain visual state – a visual state that is similar to the visual state you might be in when looking at a *mere* array of dots presented below.

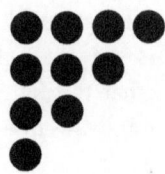

Though these two visual states – the visual state presenting the mere array and the visual state that occurs as part of grasping the proof – are similar, I find phenomenal differences between them. That is, the visual state I am in as part of the cognitive state of grasping the proof seems phenomenally different from the visual state I am in independently of my cognitive state of grasping the proof. One might argue about how to best gloss the difference, but here is one thing I would say about how the array is presented to me in the context of grasping the proof that I wouldn't say about how the mere array is presented to me: it seems to be a portion of a larger structure.

The visual state presenting the array that occurs as part of the phenomenally conscious cognitive state of grasping the proof has a distinctive phenomenal character. So much seems introspectively evident. A further claim is that this visual state depends for its phenomenal character on the cognitive state of grasping the proof – that the visual state is a part of a cognitive gestalt. This seems plausible to me on the same sorts of grounds reviewed above: I cannot imagine a phenomenally identical visual state occurring independently of a larger phenomenally conscious cognitive state of grasping the proof. When I try I wind up imagining a visual state that is phenomenally like the one that occurs when I look at the mere array. And this is clearly a phenomenally different visual state.

The implication is that sensory states that occur in the context of phenomenally conscious cognition depend on cognitive phenomenal states. This gives us further evidence against the claim that if there are cognitive phenomenal states, then they form a category that is analogous to an extra sensory modality.

The missing explanation argument

Adam Pautz raises two difficulties for Irreducibility – which he calls CP-existence, the "CP" indicating irreducible cognitive phenomenology. The first is a problem about the possibility of cognitive phenomenal states disembodied from sensory states. Here is how he puts it:

> My first argument casts doubt on the CP-existence thesis and has two steps. If there are cognitive qualia, then in the actual world they are *embodied* in the sense that they are accompanied by sensory properties, including experiences of having a body and acting on the world. The first step of my argument asserts that, if there are cognitive phenomenal properties distinct from all sensory properties, then *disembodied cognitive qualia cases* ought to be possible and indeed we should be able to positively *imagine* them. In such a case, we allegedly have a rich phenomenal life that *overlaps* with our actual phenomenal life because we have all the same cognitive phenomenal properties we have in the actual world; but our cognitive phenomenal properties are "disembodied" in the sense that they are not accompanied by any *sensory* properties.
>
> The second step of my disembodied cognitive qualia argument against the CP-existence thesis is that we *cannot* positively imagine such a case. At least *I* cannot. Just try. If the CP-existence thesis is true, then in such a case we have a rich phenomenal life that *overlaps* with our actual phenomenal life, only it is totally non-sensory. But what would it be like?

Can you imagine this overlapping phenomenology? If you try to imagine what it would be like, you might imagine seeing all black, having an experience of inner speech ("nothing much is happening"), and so on. But then you will not be imagining a case in which you have cognitive phenomenal properties but *no* sensory properties. So the CP-existence thesis makes a *false empirical predication* about what we can imagine.[14]

This argument is similar to Prinz's. But there is a difference. According to Prinz, reflection on Irreducibility gives us reason to think we could be in cognitive phenomenal states in the absence of any sensory phenomenal states. According to Pautz, reflection on Irreducibility gives us reason to think that we could be in the same cognitive phenomenal states that actually exist combined with sensory phenomenal states but in the absence of those or any other sensory phenomenal states. This is a stronger claim.

Here is how we might formulate it:

Disembodied Qualia Premise: If there are cognitive phenomenal states, then there should be pairs of phenomenally different total phenomenal states T_1 and T_2 such that: T_1 includes both sensory and cognitive phenomenal states and T_2 is the same as T_1 with respect to cognitive phenomenal states but lacks all sensory phenomenal states.

Pautz's first line of reasoning against Irreducibility, then, is that given the Disembodied Qualia Premise, Irreducibility implies possibilities that are neither actualized nor imaginable.

The second problem Pautz raises is about the possibility of phenomenal differences that are wholly due to the absence of cognitive phenomenal states. Here is how he puts it:

The first step asserts that, if there are cognitive phenomenal properties, then cases of the following kind are possible and indeed we should be able to *positively imagine* them: (i) you have *exactly* the same sensory properties and functional properties that you have in the actual case, *and yet* (ii) your phenomenal life is profoundly different from your actual phenomenal life in that you lack the phenomenal properties (namely, cognitive phenomenal properties) you actually enjoy.

The second step of the argument is that we cannot positively imagine such cases. Just try. Suppose in the actual case you hear a friend say "Let's go to the bar later" and you quickly form an image of the local bar and follow up with a question as to time. Now try to imagine a case that is completely identical to the actual case in all sensory and functional respects, and yet profoundly phenomenally different in many ways in that you lack the cognitive phenomenal properties that you allegedly actually possess. I honestly cannot do it.[15]

The main premise in this line of reasoning is similar to the Disembodied Qualia Premise, but slightly different. Here is how we might formulate it:

Absent Qualia Premise: If there are cognitive phenomenal states then there should be pairs of phenomenally different total phenomenal states T_1 and T_2 such that: T_1 includes both sensory and cognitive phenomenal states and T_2 is the same as T_1 with respect to sensory phenomenal states but lacks all cognitive phenomenal states.

Pautz's second line of reasoning against Irreducibility, then, is that given the Absent Qualia Premise, Irreducibility implies possible differences in total phenomenal states that are neither actualized nor imaginable.

Pautz's Disembodied Qualia Premise and Absent Qualia Premise play the same role as Prinz's assumption that if there are cognitive phenomenal states, then they form a category that is like an extra sensory modality. These claims connect Irreducibility to Independence or claims akin to Independence such as those articulated in the consequents of the Disembodied Qualia Premise and the Absent Qualia Premise. Their upshot is to render Irreducibility as questionable as Independence and its kin.

We have already observed some grounds for skepticism about both the Disembodied Qualia Premise and the Absent Qualia Premise. Consider the cognitive phenomenal state associated with grasping the proof that the sum of the first n positive integers is half of $n \times (n + 1)$ and call it G. Consider the visual phenomenal state associated with seeing the array of dots used in the proof and call it S. When you grasp the proof you are in a total phenomenal state that includes G and S, but there is no total phenomenal state that includes just G without S. Being in G depends on being in S. This casts doubt on the Disembodied Qualia Premise. Similarly, there is no total phenomenal state that includes just S without G. The gestalt theoretical reflections pursued in the previous section gave us reason to believe that being in S depends on being in G. This casts doubt on the Absent Qualia Premise.

A natural reply on behalf of Pautz is that even if there are some interdependent sensory and cognitive states, if Irreducibility is true, then in addition there should also be some independent cognitive phenomenal states and these are neither actualized nor imaginable. This is similar to the reply we considered on behalf of Prinz, and here again the best candidate examples of such independent cognitive phenomenal states are those associated with conscious thoughts in the narrow sense such as judging, supposing, entertaining, and recollecting. These do not have sensory parts. And, at least on the face of it, no sensory states enter into gestalt connections with them. In the case of grasping the proof that the sum of the first n positive integers is half of $n \times (n + 1)$, there is an explanation for why it is associated with interdependent sensory and cognitive phenomenal states. But for many examples of judging, supposing, entertaining, and recollecting no such explanation seems available.

Pautz considers the view that in such cases there are brute, inexplicable interdependences among cognitive and sensory phenomenal states.[16] But, as he points out, this is an unattractive view. What this suggests is that though reflection on Irreducibility itself might not motivate Independence or claims akin to Independence, reflection on Irreducibility and the absence of an explanation otherwise motivates accepting these additional conclusions. Maybe there are part-whole and gestalt connections among some cognitive and sensory phenomenal states. But at least some cognitive phenomenal states – such as those associated with conscious thoughts in the narrow sense – seem like they should be distinct existences: they do not seem like they would bear part-whole or gestalt connections to sensory phenomenal states. The contrast between the two kinds of cognitive phenomenal state – i.e. ones that seem like they would bear part-whole or gestalt connections to sensory phenomenal states and ones that seem like they should be distinct existences – is striking. And it suggests that absent some explanation otherwise, then, it is reasonable to assume that Independence and claims akin to Independence hold for those cognitive phenomenal states that seem like they should be distinct existences. This is the missing explanation argument for thinking that Irreducibility is just as questionable as Independence. In the next section I consider a possible reply.

Phenomenal Holism

According to Gestaltism some partial phenomenal states depend on whole phenomenal states to which they belong. In this section I will consider the thesis of Phenomenal Holism, which strengthens this claim. We can put it as follows:

Phenomenal Holism: All partial phenomenal states depend on the total phenomenal states to which they belong.

Phenomenal Holism is inconsistent with the Disembodied Qualia Premise and the Absent Qualia Premise.

According to the Disembodied Qualia Premise, if there are cognitive phenomenal states, then there should be pairs of phenomenally different total phenomenal states T_1 and T_2 such that: T_1 includes both sensory and cognitive phenomenal states and T_2 is the same as T_1 with respect to cognitive phenomenal states but lacks all sensory phenomenal states. But if Phenomenal Holism is true, then the cognitive phenomenal states that occur in T_1 depend on T_1, which also includes sensory phenomenal states. So there couldn't be a T_2 that included phenomenally equivalent cognitive phenomenal states without including phenomenally equivalent sensory phenomenal states.

According to the Absent Qualia Premise, if there are cognitive phenomenal states then there should be pairs of phenomenally different total phenomenal states T_1 and T_2 such that: T_1 includes both sensory and cognitive phenomenal states and T_2 is the same as T_1 with respect to sensory phenomenal states but lacks all cognitive phenomenal states. But if Phenomenal Holism is true, then the partly sensory phenomenal states that occur in T_1 depend on T_1, which also includes cognitive phenomenal states. So there couldn't be a T_2 that included phenomenally equivalent partly sensory phenomenal states without including phenomenally equivalent cognitive phenomenal states.

Phenomenal Holism is also inconsistent with Independence itself, at least when interpreted as being about actual cognitive states. According to Independence so interpreted, some actual cognitive states put one in phenomenal states that are independent of sensory states. But any actual cognitive state occurs in conjunction with sensory states. So if Phenomenal Holism is true, actual cognitive phenomenal states depend on total phenomenal states that also include sensory phenomenal states. So you couldn't have these actual cognitive phenomenal states independently of those sensory phenomenal states.

Phenomenal Holism is, however, consistent with the possibility of cognitive phenomenal states in the absence of all sensory phenomenal states. What it implies – given the fact that actual cognitive states occur in conjunction with sensory states – is that these cognitive phenomenal states never actually occur and so are ones with which no one is acquainted. The significance of this point is that even if one is convinced that Irreducibility gives us reason to believe in the possibility of cognitive phenomenal states in the absence of all sensory phenomenal states, Phenomenal Holism suggests an explanation for why we cannot imagine such cognitive phenomenal states. Our actual cognitive phenomenal states might not provide us with adequate imaginative resources. This has a consequence for Pautz's argument: even if it is correct to infer the possibility of cognitive phenomenal states in the absence of all sensory phenomenal states, it might be mistaken to rely on what one can observe or imagine in assessing this possibility.

So Phenomenal Holism has significant consequences for debates about cognitive phenomenology. Is there any reason to believe it? In the balance of this section I will consider an argument for Phenomenal Holism that derives from Aron Gurwitsch's work.

Phenomenal Holism can be thought of as the claim that total phenomenal states are gestalts. If total phenomenal states at a time are gestalts, however, they are not of the same type as occurs when you look at figure D from the second section (p. 112). Many partial phenomenal states do not depend for their phenomenally conscious content on the total phenomenal state of which they are parts. Suppose some random thought consciously occurs to you. It is implausible that it depends for its phenomenally conscious content on the total phenomenal state within which it occurs. So let us assume that it does not. Still, it might depend for its phenomenally conscious manner on the total phenomenal state within which it occurs. So total phenomenal states might be gestalts of the same type as occurs when you look at Rubin's Vase, or when you look at figure G from the second section (p. 112). This is the view that Gurwitsch defends.

Gurwitsch's view is developed over the course of his book *The Field of Consciousness*, which also touches on many issues that we cannot explore here. I will boil the relevant points down into four theses.

(A)   Total phenomenal states at a time divide into theme, thematic field, and margin.

The plausibility of (A) depends on what we mean by theme, thematic field, and margin. Here is how Gurwitsch first introduces (A):

We shall establish and substantiate the thesis that every total field of consciousness consists of three domains, each domain exhibiting a specific type of organization of its own. The first domain is the *theme*, that which engrosses the mind of the experiencing subject, or as it is often expressed, which stands in the "focus of his attention." Second is the *thematic field*, defined as the totality of those data, co-present with the theme, which are experienced as materially relevant or pertinent to the theme and form the background or horizon out of which the theme emerges as center. The third includes data which, though co-present with, have no relevancy to, the theme and comprise in their totality what we propose to call the *margin.*[17]

I will understand theme, thematic field, and margin as consisting of phenomenal states. Some phenomenal states are parts of the theme: they represent the subject's focus. Some phenomenal states are parts of the thematic field: they represent items as more or less relevant to the subject's focus. And some phenomenal states are parts of the margin: they represent items as being irrelevant to the subject's focus.

This division of phenomenal states possesses some prima facie legitimacy. The extent to which it is theoretically useful, however, depends on how it is further elaborated. The remaining theses provide this elaboration.

(B)   The relation of theme to thematic field generalizes the relation of figure to ground.

This is something Gurwitsch repeats often.[18] There are two distinct lines of generalization.

The first has to do with phenomenally conscious content. The phenomenally conscious contents of figure states and ground states exhibit some distinctive features. Recall the Rubin Vase. When the white part of the physical image appears as figure it seems to have a contour. When it appears as ground it seems to lack a contour; in this case the two black faces seem to have a contour. The same white patch appears in both phenomenal states, but it appears differently when it appears as figure than when it appears as ground. In general, figure states represent contours, and ground states do not.

This difference in phenomenally conscious content can be generalized. When something appears to have a contour it appears as a cohesive individual. But something can appear as a cohesive individual but not in virtue of appearing to have a contour, for it might not be the sort of thing that could have a contour. Consider, for example, a musical note. When something appears to lack a contour it appears as some indefinite stuff. But something can appear as some indefinite stuff but not in virtue of appearing to lack a contour, for it might not be the sort of thing that could have a contour. Consider, for example, the sounds that form the always present but seldom noticed auditory background within which we live.

So the first way the relation of theme to thematic field generalizes the relation of figure to ground is this. Theme phenomenal states represent things as cohesive individuals. Field phenomenal states represent things as indefinite stuff. This last point should be qualified. It is not as if what appears in a thematic field appears as homogenous. Suppose your auditory background includes the sound of your air conditioner and the sound of your neighbors' dog barking. These appear as different sounds. But they also appear as belonging to an ill-defined grouping of sounds. This ill-defined grouping is the indefinite stuff of your auditory background. Suppose you are attending to the news. You hear a grouping of sounds. But it is no longer ill-defined. The sounds you hear belong together and form a cohesive individual – the news report.

The second line of generalization has to do with phenomenally conscious manner. Figure states and ground states depend on each other for their phenomenal character. As discussed above, they do not depend on each other for their phenomenally conscious content. Rather, they depend on each other for the manner in which they present their phenomenally conscious content. The figure phenomenal states you are in when you represent a white vase represent that white vase in a manner that is fixed by its standing out from a specific background, which is represented by your ground phenomenal state. Similarly, the ground phenomenal state you are in when you represent a black background represents that black background in a manner that is fixed by its standing behind a specific figure, which is represented by your figure phenomenal state.

These dependencies in phenomenally conscious manner can be generalized. Here is how we might put the generalizations:

Your theme states represent their contents in phenomenally conscious manners fixed by those contents appearing in a specific context, which is represented by your field states.[19]

Your field states represent their contents in phenomenally conscious manners fixed by those contents forming the context of a specific focus, which is represented by your theme states.[20]

Here I am using the term "context" to pick out the phenomenally conscious contents of field phenomenal states. It generalizes the notion of background.

The motivation for making these generalizations comes from reflection on examples. Gurwitsch describes one involving thought.[21] Here are two different phenomenally conscious states you might be in. You might consciously entertain the thought that Columbus discovered America in 1492 in the context of thinking about great geographical discoveries in the age of exploration. Or you might consciously entertain the same thought in the context of thinking about the growth of Spanish power in the early modern period. In each case the thought that Columbus discovered America in 1492 is your theme. What differs is the thematic field. In the first it is constituted by thoughts about the growth of geographical knowledge. In the second it is constituted by thoughts about early modern politics. There is a felt difference between the two overall experiences. But this felt difference does not seem to be exhausted by the difference between your thoughts about the growth of geographical knowledge and your thoughts about early modern politics. Rather, there is a felt difference in your thought about Columbus. Following Gurwitsch we might say that it appears to you in a different perspective, light, or orientation depending on which thematic field it occurs in. Note that the content of the thought remains the same. What differs is the manner in which you represent that content. So this is a case that illustrates how the phenomenally conscious manner of a theme state might depend on the phenomenally conscious contents of the field states that make up the context in which it occurs. I discuss how the phenomenally conscious manner of field phenomenal states might depend on the contents of theme phenomenal states below.

(C)   Phenomenal states in the thematic field are experienced as comparatively more or less central to the theme.[22]

Thesis (C) tells us two things. First it tells us how the phenomenally conscious manners of field states depend on the contents of theme states. The manners in which phenomenally conscious field states represent their contents are fixed by how central those contents are experienced as being to the contents of phenomenally conscious theme states. Here is how Gurwitsch puts the idea in his dissertation:

> The ground (thematic field) is organized around the figure (theme). There is always given a thematic field organized and oriented with respect to this theme. Whatever is experienced as pertaining to the thematic field has "directedness to the center."[23]

The second thing thesis (C) tells us is that phenomenal states in the thematic field can be *ordered* by experienced comparative centrality:

> Not all items pertaining to the ground have the same relationship to the figure. Material relations may differ from one another: they may, for example, be more or less close. Along with them there is variation in the position which the components of the thematic field occupy with respect to the theme ... In such ways nearer and further zones are delimited within the thematic field, according to the closer and looser material relations between its items and the theme.[24]

How comparatively central a field state seems to the theme can be fixed in different ways.

One way is by the spatial relations that appear to hold between the theme state's focus and items in the field. Suppose you examine a house. It stands out from its surroundings. Your experience of the house is your theme phenomenal state. Your experiences of its surroundings are your field phenomenal states. The surroundings can be ordered by their proximity to the house. And this ordering is one way to induce an ordering of comparative centrality on the field states: one field state is more central to the theme than another field state just in case what it represents appears to be in greater spatial proximity to the house than does what the other represents.

Apparent spatial relations do not provide the only way to induce an ordering of comparative centrality on field states. Take events in a narrative, such as *Hamlet*. Suppose you consider Claudius's departure during the murder scene of *The Murder of Gonzago*. This is the event you focus on. You also have other events in mind – for example, the events leading up to the staging of the play, such as Hamlet's conversation with the ghost of his father, and the events that ensue after Hamlet observes Claudius's departure. These events form the background out of which Claudius's departure emerges. They stand in relations of more or less narrative relevance to Claudius's departure. And this relation of narrative relevance might induce a relation of comparative centrality on the field phenomenal states partly in virtue of which you consciously represent them.

Field states can be ordered by comparative centrality to the theme even in the absence of any spatial, temporal, or causal structure. Suppose you are working through a proof. As you focus on one step in the proof, it will stand out from a background consisting of other steps in the proof. These steps appear as more or less immediate premises in the establishment of or consequences of the step you focus on. The field states partly in virtue of which you consciously represent them can be ordered by the relation of comparative centrality to the theme in a way that respects this order of apparent inferential relations.

In addition to theme states and field states, there are marginal phenomenal states. The need for these should be clear. Suppose you are looking at a house. It emerges from a background that your field states represent. Now suppose some random thought about recent politics occurs to you. This thought has no relevance to the house. It is in the margin. This example might not work for everyone. If you are passionate about recent politics, thoughts about it might in fact color your other phenomenal states, no matter what their contents. Perhaps this is because thoughts about recent politics influence your mood and moods somehow color all phenomenal states. Even if this example does not work to introduce the notion of a marginal state for you, however, I will assume that some example or other will.

(D)   Phenomenal states in the margin are experienced as comparatively least central to the theme.

Gurwitsch says that states in the margin are "characterized by their *irrelevancy* to both the theme and the thematic field with which they are co-present."[25] This can be interpreted in two ways. On one interpretation, phenomenal states in the margin do not stand in a relation of comparative centrality to the theme. It is undefined for them; marginal states are not in its domain or range – not in its field. On another interpretation phenomenal states in the margin do stand in a relation of comparative centrality to the theme. What distinguishes them is that they are comparatively least central to the theme: marginal states are those that are no more central to the theme than any other phenomenal state is.

I favor the second interpretation. There are two reasons why. First, it tells us what positive property endows marginal states with their distinctively marginal character. Just saying that they lack a certain property possessed by other phenomenal states does not do this. Second, it allows us to define the field of consciousness. The field of consciousness is just the field of the comparative centrality relation. We can do more. Taking the relation of comparative centrality to the theme as our single primitive, we can give a rigorous characterization of the structure of the field of consciousness.

Here is how.[26] Let us call the comparative-centrality-to-the-theme relation *centrality* for short, and when a phenomenal state X bears it to Y, we will say

"X is more central than Y." We can assume that it is a strict partial ordering. Taking it as our primitive we can define theme, field, and margin:

- X is in the theme = $_{df}$ for all Y, Y is not more central than X (i.e. X is a minimal element of the centrality ordering)
- X is in the margin = $_{df}$ for all Y, X is not more central than Y (i.e. X is a maximal element of the centrality ordering)
- X is in the field = $_{df}$ for some Y and some Z, Y is more central than X and X is more general than Z (i.e. X is neither minimal nor maximal).

We can distill much of the import of theses (A) through (D) into two claims. The first tells us about the field of the centrality relation:

- Every field includes a theme, field, and margin.

The second thesis tells us about the phenomenal significance of the centrality relation:

- For all X and Y, if X is more central than Y, then this makes a difference to the phenomenally conscious manners of X and Y.

These two claims do not contain all of the content of theses (A) through (D). They contain that content which is required for the argument for Phenomenal Holism.

That argument requires a new relation, which can be defined in terms of the centrality relation just introduced. The centrality relation is taken as primitive. And the new relation is best defined in two stages. Here they are:

Centrality Related: X is centrality related to Y = $_{df}$ X is more central than Y or Y is more central than X.

Centrality Connected: X is centrality connected to Y = $_{df}$ there is a sequence of states X, e_1, ... , e_n, Y whose first member is X and whose last member is Y and is such that adjacent states are centrality related – in brief: there is a path from X to Y through centrality-related phenomenal states.

Now we can argue for Phenomenal Holism as follows:

(1)   A phenomenal state has its location in the centrality ordering because of its centrality connections to other phenomenal states. [Premise]

(2) Every phenomenal state is centrality connected to every other phenomenal state – i.e. given any two phenomenal states X and Y in a total phenomenal state at a time, X and Y are centrality connected. [Premise]

(3) A phenomenal state has its location in the centrality ordering because of its centrality connections to every other phenomenal state. [From (1) and (2)]

(4) A phenomenal state has its phenomenal character in part because of its location in the centrality ordering (e.g. whether it is in the theme, field, or margin). [Premise]

(5) A phenomenal state has its phenomenal character in part because of its centrality connections to every other phenomenal state. [From (3) and (4)]

(6) A phenomenal state has its phenomenal character essentially. [Premise]

(7) A phenomenal state depends for its occurrence on its centrality connections to every other phenomenal state in the total phenomenal state to which it belongs. [From (5) and (6)]

(8) If a phenomenal state depends for its occurrence on its centrality connections to every other phenomenal state in the total phenomenal state to which it belongs, then it depends for its occurrence on the total phenomenal state to which it belongs. [Premise]

(9) So, a phenomenal state depends for its occurrence on the total phenomenal state to which it belongs. [From (7) and (8)]

Since (9) is about an arbitrary experience it implies Phenomenal Holism – that all partial phenomenal states of a subject at a time depend on the subject's total phenomenal state at that time.

(1), (2), (4), (6), and (8) are the independent premises. I will assume (6) and (8). Both seem plausible to me. (1) is motivated by the thought that there is nothing else to account for a phenomenal state's location in the centrality ordering.

The usefulness of introducing the relation of centrality connectedness is precisely its role in motivating (2). Notice that similar claims about centrality or centrality relatedness are not necessarily true. You might have two field states each of which is more or less central to the theme, but neither of which is more or less central than the other to the theme. But given that every phenomenal state in the field of consciousness is in the field of the centrality relation and given that the centrality relation has minimal and maximal elements – i.e. the phenomenal states in the theme and the phenomenal states in the margin – it follows that there is always a path from any one phenomenal state to another through centrality-related phenomenal states. (4) is motivated by the earlier discussion of Gurwitsch.

Summary

So that is the argument for Phenomenal Holism. If Phenomenal Holism is true, then it gives us reason to separate commitment to Irreducibility from commitment to Independence. If it is not true, however, then Independence might be a viable thesis about at least some actual cognitive phenomenal states, particularly those associated with conscious thoughts in the narrow sense that pop into mind here and there. Either way there is no good reason to reject Irreducibility as a thesis about some phenomenal states.

Notes

1 Prinz 2011, 193.
2 McGurk and MacDonald 1976.
3 Wertheimer's "Gestalt Theory," in Ellis 1938.
4 The example is based on one from Wertheimer's "Laws of Organization in Perceptual Forms," in Ellis 1938.
5 The quoted formulation is from Koffka 1935, 110.
6 Gurwitsch 1964, 121.
7 For an illuminating discussion of these matters from a psychological perspective see Palmer 1990.
8 Section 6 of the dissertation reprinted in Gurwitsch 1966.
9 See Koffka 1935, 184–185, for a fuller discussion of this point.
10 Gurwitsch 1964, 357.
11 This distinction is adapted from Chalmers' (2004) distinction between pure and impure representational properties.
12 See, for example, Gurwitsch 1964, 456, where he distinguishes between "*the proposition which is apprehended* and *the proposition taken as it is apprehended.*" Italics in the original.
13 See Gurwitsch 1964, 327, 359, and 363. In these discussions Gurwitsch draws the same distinction between content and manner I have drawn except he uses Husserlian jargon, and he applies the distinction in the same way I have applied it except he does so to the more general case of theme and thematic field, about which see below.
14 Pautz 2013, 219.

15 Ibid., 216.

16 Ibid., 215.

17 Gurwitsch 1964, 4.

18 See, for example, ibid., 113, 320–321, and 356–357.

19 See ibid., 319: "The *appearance of a theme* must be described as *emergence from a field* in which the theme is located occupying the center so that the field forms a background with respect to the theme. The theme carries a field along with it so as not to appear and be present to consciousness except as being in, and pointing to, the field." Italics in original.

20 See ibid., 340: "Dealing with a scientific theorem, we have a more or less explicit and clear consciousness of what leads to that theorem, of consequences of this theorem, of other theorems compatible or incompatible with it, of facts somehow related to those to which our theorem refers ... the data falling in [this] class [i.e. the field] appear, moreover, as *being of a certain concern* to the theme." Italics in original.

21 See ibid., 359.

22 Gurwitsch uses the term "relevance" for what I am calling centrality. See, for example, ibid., 340–341.

23 Ibid., 204.

24 Ibid., 205.

25 Ibid., 344.

26 See Watzl 2011.

Further reading

See Prinz (2011) and Pautz (2013) for the arguments against Irreducibility considered in this chapter. Good places to start exploring issues about gestalts and Phenomenal Holism are: Ellis (1938), Gurwitsch (1964), Palmer (1990), and Dainton (2000/2006). Watzl (2011) develops a theory of attention that is close to Gurwitsch's theory of the field of conscious.

6

INTENTIONALITY

Suppose you consciously think that there is mail in your mailbox. Then you are in a phenomenal state. There is something it is like for you when you think that there is mail in your mailbox. You are also in a cognitive intentional state. There is a way that you cognitively represent the world as being when you think that there is mail in your mailbox. So the conscious thought has both phenomenal and cognitive intentional aspects. How might these be related?

One view is that the phenomenal state determines the cognitive intentional state. On this view, consciously thinking that there is mail in your mailbox provides an instance of the Cognitive Phenomenal Intentionality thesis, which says that some phenomenal states determine cognitive intentional states. This is the thesis that I will be concerned with in this chapter.

The view that the phenomenal state you are in when you think that there is mail in your mailbox determines the cognitive intentional state you are in when you think that there is mail in your mailbox contrasts with two others. The first is the view that the two states do not bear determination relations to each other. And the second is the view that they do, but it is the cognitive intentional state that determines the phenomenal state rather than the phenomenal state that determines the cognitive intentional state. It is difficult to say anything about the relative merits of these different views without first considering how they might be elaborated. This project lies beyond the scope of my present ambitions.

My aim here is simply to clarify the issues relevant to assessing the merits of Cognitive Phenomenal Intentionality on its own. And I emphasize that it is Cognitive Phenomenal Intentionality specifically that I am concerned with, not the more general Phenomenal Intentionality thesis, according to which some phenomenal states determine intentional states – where these intentional states might not be cognitive intentional states.

There are four main questions I will take up: How should the determination relation Cognitive Phenomenal Intentionality says some phenomenal states bear to cognitive intentional states be understood? What reasons are there to believe the thesis? What difficulties does it face? In light of the difficulties facing Cognitive Phenomenal Intentionality what options are there for proponents of it? Each section below is dedicated to one of these questions. My own view is that the status of Cognitive Phenomenal Intentionality remains an open question.

Grounding or Necessitation

The Cognitive Phenomenal Intentionality thesis leaves open the nature of the determination relation it says some phenomenal states bear to cognitive intentional states. There are two main options for making this aspect of the thesis more definite. These are the following:

Grounding: Some phenomenal states put one in a cognitive intentional state.

Necessitation: Some phenomenal states suffice for being in a cognitive intentional state.

We can make the difference between these clearer by focusing on what they imply about explanation. If we adopt Grounding, then we are committed to the idea that sometimes it is because you are in a phenomenal state that you are in a cognitive intentional state. If we adopt Necessitation, then we are not committed to the idea that sometimes it is because you are in a phenomenal state that you are a cognitive intentional state.

There are reasons for and against each option.

Consider Grounding first. The main attraction of Grounding is that it suggests a diagnosis of and a repair to an apparent gap in our understanding of meaning and intentionality. This apparent gap emerged in the course of two lines of investigation. The first was the project of addressing worries about the determinacy of meaning and intentionality raised most prominently in the works of Quine and Kripke. The second was the project of naturalizing meaning and intentionality.

Suppose, as we might naively put it, you mean to refer to a rabbit by uttering the words "Lo, a rabbit!" Presumably this fact about you is not basic. It depends on other facts about you. According to Quine the only facts on which it can depend are facts about your publicly observable dispositions to use the words "Lo, a rabbit!"[1] But these fail to distinguish between the following interpretations of your utterance: you mean to refer to a rabbit, you mean to refer to an undetached rabbit part, or you mean to refer to a temporal part of a rabbit's life. If you have publicly observable dispositions to utter the words "Lo, a rabbit!" whenever there is a rabbit about, then those same publicly observable dispositions are dispositions to utter the words "Lo, a rabbit!" whenever there is an undetached rabbit part about or whenever there is a temporal part of a rabbit's life about. Quine concludes that our naive claim that you mean to refer to a rabbit by uttering the words "Lo, a rabbit!" is mistaken. Your utterance does not have a determinate meaning. This skeptical conclusion ramifies: presumably if you could determinately intend to refer to a rabbit, then you could determinately refer to a rabbit, but since you cannot do the latter, you cannot do the former, and this suggests that determinate intentional states are as illusory as determinately meaningful utterances. In his work on Wittgenstein, Kripke develops a similar line of reasoning, though unlike Quine he does not restrict the potential determinants of meaning and intentionality to publicly observable dispositions.[2]

The project of naturalizing meaning and intentionality also begins with the thought that facts about what one means by utterances and facts about what intentional states one is in are not basic.[3] They depend on other facts. The idea behind the project is that these other facts must be in some sense natural. They must be facts about one's physical constitution, dispositions, history, and environment. The project is to make this idea plausible by giving necessary and sufficient conditions for meaning and intentionality in terms of physical constitution, dispositions, history, and environment. If this project were successfully carried out, then it would result in an answer to the skeptical worries raised by Quine and Kripke. But this does not seem to have happened, at least not with any consensus.

Cognitive Phenomenal Intentionality construed as a thesis about grounding suggests both a diagnosis of and a repair to the situation.[4] The diagnosis is that Quine, Kripke, and the naturalizers have ignored an important set of facts on which facts about meaning and intentionality depend, namely facts about phenomenal states. The repair is to stop ignoring these facts.

So much for the attraction of Grounding. The problem with Grounding is that it leaves the nature of the phenomenal states that are supposed to ground cognitive intentional states a complete mystery. One wants to know: what are these states? A tempting idea is that they just are cognitive intentional states. They are states that are both phenomenal and cognitive intentional – i.e. phenomenal cognitive intentional states. But Grounding seems to foreclose this option. To see this, recall that the grounding relation is irreflexive: nothing grounds itself. So suppose some phenomenal state P grounds some cognitive intentional state C. By the irreflexivity of grounding, P is not identical to C. So we can't explain what P is by saying it is just C itself.

There are two possible replies to this argument. One is to challenge the irreflexivity of grounding.[5] Another is to suggest that while P might not be identical to C, it might be identical to some other phenomenal cognitive intentional state, call it C*. All irreflexivity rules out is that a phenomenal state is identical to any of the cognitive intentional states it grounds. Irreflexivity does not rule out the possibility that a phenomenal state is identical to some other cognitive intentional state it does not ground. The picture, then, would be that some phenomenal cognitive intentional states ground other cognitive intentional states. It implies that at least some cognitive intentional states are not grounded in – though they might be identical to – phenomenal states.[6] It seems premature to rule out either of these options. Maybe one of them will prove workable.

The nice thing about Necessitation is that it does clearly allow us to say that the phenomenal states that determine cognitive intentional states just are cognitive intentional states. Unlike grounding, necessitation is reflexive: everything necessitates itself. So suppose some phenomenal state P necessitates some cognitive intentional state C. P might very well be C. In fact, the identity of P and C would give us a good idea of just how it is that P necessitates C. P necessitates C because everything necessitates itself and P just is C.

The problem with combining Necessitation with the view that those phenomenal states and cognitive intentional states for which it holds are identical is that the result seems to rule out any explanatory ambitions. Maybe it is a good thing to know that some phenomenal states are cognitive intentional states. Now we know more about the nature of these phenomenal states. But this does nothing to diagnose or repair the apparent gap in our understanding that emerged in the literature on skepticism and naturalism about meaning and intentionality. For, on this view, phenomenal cognitive intentional states are an addition to what needs the grounding not an addition to what does the grounding. So there is no diagnosis because we haven't been told what possible grounds we've been over-looking. And there is no repair because we haven't been provided with any new possible grounds to work with.

Someone more sanguine about the advances represented by the new focus on cognitive phenomenal intentionality might argue that cognitive phenomenal intentional states do not need grounding. Their intentionality is special because it is phenomenally manifest. You can't doubt it because it is there to be experienced. You can't ground it because it is primitively built into phenomenology. I am sympathetic to both claims. But I do not see how they are new moves in the dialectic. Anti-reductionism and anti-skepticism are positions that have been available all along.[7] It is not clear how Cognitive Phenomenal Intentionality taken as a claim about necessitation adds anything to them.

Arguments for Cognitive Phenomenal Intentionality

Bracketing the question of how exactly to understand the relevant deter-mination relation, we can ask: why think some phenomenal states bear any such relation to cognitive intentional states? In this section I will consider two argumentative strategies, both neutral with respect to the Grounding vs. Necessitation issue. The first proceeds via reflection on phenomenal contrast cases. The second proceeds via reflection on imagined scenarios.

Tim Bayne pursues an argument of the first sort for thinking that pheno-menal intentionality extends to intentional states representing high-level properties such as natural and artifactual kinds. This is not our focus here, but it will prove instructive to examine his argument since it is a clear illustration of the argumentative strategy in question. Bayne reflects on a phenomenal contrast due to associative agnosia. Victims of associative agnosia are able to see color and shape but are not able to visually recognize natural and artifactual kinds. After quoting a description of such a case from the psychological literature, Bayne writes:

> Associative agnosia provides a tool with which to develop a potent con-trast argument for liberalism [i.e. the view that phenomenal intentionality extends to high-level properties]. Although we have no direct access to

the patient's phenomenal state, it is extremely plausible to suppose that the phenomenal character of his visual experience has changed. But what kind of perceptual content has the patient lost? He has not lost low-level perceptual content, for those abilities that require the processing of only low-level content remain intact. The patient's deficit is not one of *form* perception but of *category* perception. Hence high-level perceptual representation – the representation of an object as a stethoscope, a can-opener or a comb – can enter into the contents of perceptual phenomenality [i.e. content determined by perceptual phenomenology].[8]

The idea seems to be this. There are two experiences e_1 and e_2. They differ phenomenally: e_2 puts one in a different phenomenal state from e_1. The best explanation for this is that they differ intentionally: e_2 puts one in a different intentional state from e_1 – in particular an intentional state that represents some artifactual kinds. Therefore the phenomenal state e_2 puts one in determines the intentional state e_2 puts one in, and so phenomenal intentionality extends to the representation of artifactual kinds.

Now just substitute your favorite phenomenal contrast case from chapter 2 or elsewhere and you have an argument for thinking that phenomenal intentionality extends to cognitive intentional states. Let's use Strawson's phenomenal contrast case involving Jacques and Jack. Jack hears the news without understanding. Jacques hears the news with understanding. There are two experiences e_1 and e_2. Experience e_2 puts one in a different phenomenal state from e_1. The best explanation for this is that e_2 puts one in a different cognitive intentional state from e_1. Therefore the phenomenal state e_2 puts one in determines the intentional state e_2 puts one in, and so phenomenal intentionality extends to cognitive phenomenal intentionality.

The problem with this argument is that the conclusion doesn't follow from the premises. From the premise that e_2 phenomenally differs from e_1 because e_2 intentionally differs from e_1 it does not follow that e_2's phenomenal character determines e_2's intentional content. This point is instructive about phenomenal intentionality in general regardless of questions about its scope. In general, premises establishing that some intentional differences determine phenomenal differences do not warrant conclusions claiming that some phenomenal differences determine intentional differences.

At least they do not do so without supplementation. In the course of arguing *against* the view that phenomenal intentionality extends to intentional states representing high-level properties, Berit Brogaard isolates the sort of supplementation that would work. She calls it the Property Supervenience Thesis:

> If S has an experience E with phenomenology C, and S is phenomenally conscious of P in virtue of having E, then necessarily, if someone has an experience with phenomenology C, then they are phenomenally conscious of P in virtue of having that experience.[9]

Consider e_2 again – either from Bayne's phenomenal contrast or from Strawson's phenomenal contrast. The state e_2 has some "phenomenology C." That is, it puts one in some phenomenal state. And e_2 makes one "phenomenally conscious of P." That is, it puts one in some intentional state part of whose content represents the property P. Now suppose the Property Supervenience Thesis is true. Then it follows that "phenomenology C" determines being "phenomenally conscious of P." That is, the phenomenal state e_2 puts one in determines the intentional state e_2 puts one in. And this is exactly the conclusion we were looking for.

The Property Supervenience Thesis, however, is problematic. On the face of it, from the fact that an experience with a certain phenomenal character makes one conscious of a certain property, it does not follow that that experience's phenomenal character is of a sort to determine that any other experience with it will also make one conscious of that same property. Brogaard sketches an argument for thinking that it does follow.[10] The main idea is that there could be a first human being who consciously represents property P in virtue of an illusory experience as of something being P; so the fact that this person consciously represents property P just depends on the phenomenal character of the experience. The argument is a bit quick. It could be that the first human who represents property P can do so because he or she can define P in terms of other properties he or she has veridically experienced. Or it could be that the first human who represents property P can do so because of the maturation of an innate capacity to represent P. But suppose we rule these sorts of explanation out. Then the argument is just as dubious as the Property Supervenience Thesis itself. If someone has an illusory experience as of something being P, then that person consciously represents property P. But one wants some reason to think a human being in the imagined circumstances can have an illusory experience as of something being P.

We might imagine such a human being having an experience with the same phenomenal character as an actual experience as of something being P. But the question is whether what we have imagined is also a human being having an experience as of something being P. It is difficult to see why this must be so in general. But perhaps it works for certain specific experiences. This possibility suggests pursuing the second argumentative strategy for drawing conclusions about phenomenal intentionality.

The second argumentative strategy does not depend on general principles such as the Property Supervenience Premise. Rather, it proceeds via reflection on specific imagined scenarios. Here, for example, is an argument Siewert gives:

> First, consider some instance of its seeming to you as it does for it to look as if something is shaped and situated in a certain way, such as its seeming to you just as it does on a given occasion for it to look as if there is something X-shaped in a certain position. If it seems this way to you, then it appears to follow that it does look to you as if there is something X-shaped in a certain position. If this is right, then its seeming this way to you is a feature in virtue of which you are assessable for accuracy – that is to say, it is an intentional feature.[11]

Siewert picks out a certain phenomenal state – the phenomenal state associated with its looking to you as if there is something X-shaped in a certain location. He asks us to imagine you are in this phenomenal state. And then he notes that this imaginative endeavor itself suffices for imagining you as also being in an intentional state – an intentional state whose accuracy depends on there being something X-shaped in a certain location. This suggests that the phenomenal state determines the intentional state.

The same argumentative strategy can be applied toward motivating Cognitive Phenomenal Intentionality.[12] To see this we need to pick the right phenomenal state as an object of our imaginative endeavor. Consider an example discussed above:

> [Intuiting] In a book you read, "If $a < 1$, then $2 - 2a > 0$," and you wonder whether this is true. Then you "see" how a's being less than 1 makes $2a$ smaller than 2 and so $2 - 2a$ greater than 0.

Intuiting an arithmetical truth is a cognitive intentional state. It is also phenomenally conscious. Call the phenomenal state it puts you in P. Could one be in that very phenomenal state P and not be in any intentional state whatsoever? Initially at least, it is difficult to see how. Could one be in P and not be in any cognitive intentional state? Initially at least, I'm inclined to think no. It does seem to me that in imagining a subject being in P I thereby imagine a subject who is engaging in some form of cognition. The subject might not really intuit an arithmetical truth. Perhaps that achievement requires more than being in a certain phenomenal state. Even so, there is a seeming intuition. The subject seems to be grasping some abstract truth. This might not be the same exact cognitive intentional state as occurs in the actual scenario, but it is a cognitive intentional state of some sort.

I think this argument gives us a prima facie reason to believe Cognitive Phenomenal Intentionality. Whether this prima facie reason stands up under scrutiny, however, is not so clear. I discuss problems for Cognitive Phenomenal Intentionality in the next section.

A problem for Cognitive Phenomenal Intentionality

In "The Intentionality of Phenomenology and the Phenomenology of Intentionality," Horgan and Tienson give the following argument:

> Phenomenology is *narrow*, in the sense that it does not depend constitutively on what's outside the skin, or indeed on what's outside of the brain. We can now make the central argument:
>
> (1) There is pervasive intentional content that constitutively depends on phenomenology alone.
> (2) Phenomenology constitutively depends only on narrow factors.
>
> So,
>
> (3) There is pervasive intentional content that constitutively depends only on narrow factors.
>
> That is, the theses of phenomenal intentionality and the narrowness of phenomenology jointly entail that there is [a] kind of *narrow* intentional content (the kind we have dubbed *phenomenal* intentional content), pervasive in human life, such that any two creatures who are phenomenal duplicates must also have exactly similar intentional states vis-à-vis this kind of narrow content.[13]

So goes the *modus ponens* that proponents of phenomenal intentionality are inclined to accept. Opponents, however, will demur, offering the predictable *modus tollens*: there is no pervasive intentional content that constitutively depends on narrow factors alone, phenomenology constitutively depends on narrow factors, so there is no pervasive intentional content that constitutively depends on phenomenology alone.

Here it is worth taking note of a crucial clarification that Horgan and Tienson add in another part of their paper.[14] The clarification is that the conclusion of their argument should be strengthened to the following: there is pervasive intentional content that constitutively depends only on phenomenal states. This is unsurprising, for if phenomenal states determine intentional states then those intentional states constitutively depend only on phenomenal states. But it is also very significant. Since people in different brain states can be in the same phenomenal state, many "narrow factors" will not be narrow enough to have any bearing on those intentional states determined by phenomenal states. It is important to keep this in mind when assessing the plausibility of phenomenal intentionality.

The main problem for Cognitive Phenomenal Intentionality, then, is that there are good reasons to think that in general cognitive intentional states fail to constitutively depend on phenomenal states alone. This is a familiar worry. But I suspect proponents of Cognitive Phenomenal Intentionality have underestimated its force. The aim of this section is to try to make that force clearer.

I will assume that it makes sense to classify intentional states in terms of their involving representational capacities akin to those involved in the usage of various categories of linguistic expression. Suppose you think that Gödel proved the Incompleteness Theorem. This is an intentional state. I am not assuming that in order to be in this intentional state you must use the name "Gödel." But I am assuming that it makes sense to say of this intentional state that it presupposes a representational capacity akin to that involved in using the name "Gödel." We might call this capacity a nominal concept and say that the intentional state involves a nominal concept for Gödel. Suppose you are standing next to Gödel and think that that man proved the Incompleteness Theorem. In this case you are not in an intentional state that presupposes a representational capacity akin to that involved in using the name "Gödel." Rather, you are in an intentional state that presupposes a representational capacity akin to that involved in using the demonstrative expression "that man." We might call this a demonstrative concept and say that the intentional state involves a demonstrative concept.

In outline the argument against Cognitive Phenomenal Intentionality can be put like this:

(1)   Every cognitive intentional state involves at least one or another of the following sorts of concepts: demonstrative, indexical, nominal, natural, mathematical, artifactual, social, normative, or logical.

(2)   Cognitive intentional states that involve demonstrative, indexical, nominal, natural, mathematical, artifactual, social, normative, or logical concepts do not constitutively depend on phenomenal states alone.

(3)   So phenomenal states fail to determine cognitive intentional states – i.e. Cognitive Phenomenal Intentionality is false.

I will discuss each premise in turn. But first I will say what I mean by the different concepts mentioned in them.

By demonstrative, indexical, and nominal concepts I have in mind representational capacities akin to those involved in the usage of terms such as "that man," "this," "I," "here," "now," "Gödel," and "Churchill." When we exercise these representational capacities we get into intentional states that are naturally expressed in language using these expressions. Such intentional states represent particular objects – some present, some absent, some internal to our minds, and some external to our minds.

By natural and mathematical concepts I have in mind representational capacities akin to those involved in the usage of terms such as "water," "tiger," "heat," "curve," "polyhedron," and "function." When we exercise these representational capacities we get into intentional states that represent natural and mathematical kinds. There are two significant features of such kinds. The first is that they have underlying natures. Water, for example, has observable properties such as being clear, drinkable, and present in lakes and oceans. But it also has the underlying nature of being H_2O. Polyhedra have the observable properties of being three-dimensional figures with flat faces, straight edges, and sharp corners. But they also have an underlying nature the specification of which can get rather complicated.[15] The second significant feature is that one does not need to know about the underlying nature of a natural or mathematical kind in order to have and exercise a concept for it. As mathematicians gradually uncovered the underlying nature of polyhedra, they were thinking about those very figures all along.

By artifactual and social concepts I have in mind representational capacities akin to those involved in the usage of terms such as "pencil," "sofa," "brisket," "department chair," "contract," and "dollar." When we exercise these representational capacities we get into intentional states that represent kinds the delineation of which depends on intentions, conventions, laws, institutions, and the like. These concepts are similar to the natural and mathematical kinds in that one does not need to know much about the intentions, conventions, laws, and institutions on which they depend in order to have and exercise concepts for them.

Finally, by normative and logical concepts I have in mind representational capacities akin to those involved in the usage of terms such as "ought," "cruel," "irrational," "if," "some," and "entails." A word about logical concepts is in order. Really there are two different roles these might play. Consider two different intentional states. First, take the judgment that some claim (e.g. Cognitive Phenomenal Intentionality) entails another claim, e.g. Irreducibility. In making this judgment you exercise a concept of entailment by predicating it of some pair of claims. Second, take the judgment that some version of Cognitive Phenomenal Intentionality is true. In making this judgment you do not exercise a concept of existential quantification by predicating it of anything. You exercise it just by making a judgment of a certain form, namely the form of an existential quantification. By intentional states involving logical concepts I have in mind both phenomena. My reason for putting normative and logical concepts together is that they seem to be characterized by the roles that intentional states involving them play in practical and theoretical reasoning.

What premise (1) says is that given any cognitive intentional state, it will involve representational capacities of at least one of the above sorts. One might try to give an a priori argument for this. Maybe it is a necessary truth that every cognitive intentional state has an intentional content with some logical form or other. But then this will shift all of the focus to logical concepts. Rather, I present premise (1) as something that will seem obvious on reflection. What could our cognitive intentional states be about if they are not about the sorts of things I just reviewed?

Premise (2) can be supported by reflection on pairs of cases in which there are phenomenal duplicates differing in some non-phenomenal way that seems to make a difference to what cognitive intentional states they are in. These pairs of cases and the judgments we are inclined to make about them give us reason to think the cognitive intentional states that figure in them constitutively depend on factors other than phenomenal states. There are four familiar kinds of reasoning along these lines, distinguished both by the sort of concepts targeted and the sort of extra-phenomenal dependence supported.

One line of reasoning targets demonstrative, indexical, and nominal concepts and purports to establish their object-dependence.[16] Here are two cases:

Case 1: Pointing toward lizard L_1, Alice thinks to herself: that is a flat-tailed horned lizard.

Case 2: In the same phenomenal state, pointing toward a distinct but similar looking lizard L_2, Alice thinks to herself: that is a flat-tailed horned lizard.

Alice's thought in Case 1 is true just in case L_1 is a flat-tailed horned lizard. Alice's thought in Case 2 is true just in case L_2 is a flat-tailed horned lizard. So Alice thinks different things even though she is in the same phenomenal state. It is easy to imagine variants on the cases in which Alice thinks indexical or nominal thoughts instead of demonstrative thoughts. So there is reason to think that cognitive intentional states that involve demonstrative, indexical, or nominal concepts do not constitutively depend on phenomenal states alone.

One might worry about this way of putting the conclusion, since it will not be true if the demonstrative, indexical, or nominal concepts are concepts for phenomenal states. For example, Alice might attend to an itch and think to herself: that type of experience is annoying. In this case, if you duplicate the phenomenal state you duplicate the object so even if Alice's thought is object-dependent it still might constitutively depend on phenomenal states alone. In light of this observation, we can simply revise the conclusion above to: there is reason to think that cognitive intentional states that involve demonstrative, indexical, or nominal concepts for things other than phenomenal states do not constitutively depend on phenomenal states alone.

A second line of reasoning targets natural and mathematical concepts and purports to establish their dependence on an underlying nature.[17] Putnam's Twin Earth thought experiment is an example.[18] Here are two cases:

Case 3: On Earth where the underlying nature of the watery stuff is H_2O, Oscar thinks a thought he expresses by saying, "water is clear."

Case 4: On Twin Earth where the underlying nature of the watery stuff is XYZ, Twin Oscar, who is a phenomenal duplicate of Oscar, thinks a thought he expresses by saying, "water is clear."

Oscar's thought in Case 3 is true just in case H_2O is clear. Twin Oscar's thought in Case 4 is true just in case XYZ is clear. So they think different things even though they are in the same phenomenal state.

One might wonder whether cases can be constructed to illustrate the point for mathematical rather than natural kinds. I think they can be. Consider, for example, these two cases:

Case 5: On Earth where the underlying nature of curve-like figures is to be continuous mappings of the unit interval, Oscar thinks a thought he expresses by saying, "all curves are differentiable somewhere."

Case 6: On Twin Earth where the underlying nature of curve-like figures is to be continuous mappings of the unit interval expressible by a polynomial, Twin Oscar, who is a phenomenal duplicate of Oscar, thinks a thought he expresses by saying, "all curves are differentiable somewhere."

Oscar's thought in Case 5 is true just in case all continuous mappings of the unit interval are differentiable somewhere. That means given any curve there is always some point on the curve that has a tangent. Or if you think of curves as paths of particles, then given any such path, there is always some point on the path at which the particle is traveling at some velocity. Surprisingly, this turns out to be false. Twin Oscar's thought in Case 6 is true just in case all continuous mappings of the unit interval that are expressible by a polynomial are differentiable somewhere. This turns out to be true.

In order to make the thought experiment more compelling, it might help to make two stipulations and one optional alteration. The alteration is to replace the condition of being expressible by a polynomial with some fancier condition that allows more complicated curves. The fancier the replacement the more plausible the stipulations I consider will be. But I will stick with talking about being expressible by a polynomial because polynomials are familiar. The first stipulation, then, is that all the curve-like figures Oscar and Twin Oscar are acquainted with are expressible by polynomials. The second stipulation is to suppose that Twin Earth in Case 6 is not a genuinely possible world; rather it is an impossible world in which all the continuous mappings of the unit interval that exist are expressible by polynomials. I do not see any reason to resist using impossible worlds in constructing thought experiments aimed at exploring claims about constitutive dependence. In fact, this is a familiar strategy in philosophy. Suppose God's will is necessary and truths about the good are necessary. Still we can see that truths about the good are not constitutively dependent on God's will by considering the counter-possible conditional: had God willed differently, would the truths about the good have been different? They would not, and so truths about the good are not constitutively dependent on God's will. This seems like OK reasoning to me. I don't see why we can't also appeal to counter-possible reasoning when developing Twin Earth thought experiments.

The upshot of the foregoing, then, is this: there is reason to think that cognitive intentional states that involve natural and mathematical concepts do not constitutively depend on phenomenal states alone.

A third line of reasoning targets artifactual and social concepts and purports to establish their dependence on the social environment.[19] Burge's arthritis thought experiment is an example.[20] Here are two cases:

> Case 7: In the actual world, where experts use "arthritis" to pick out rheumatoid ailments in joints, Beth visits her doctor and expresses a worry she has by saying, "I have arthritis in my thigh."

> Case 8: In a counterfactual scenario, in the same phenomenal state but living in a society in which experts use "arthritis" to pick out rheumatoid ailments in general, Beth visits her doctor and expresses a worry she has by saying, "I have arthritis in my thigh."

In Case 7, Beth's worry is mistaken, for it is well founded just in case she has arthritis in her thigh, and arthritis cannot occur there. In Case 8, Beth's worry might not be mistaken, for it is well founded just in case she has an ailment distinct from arthritis in her thigh, and this other ailment might very well occur there. So Beth has different worries even though she is in the same phenomenal state. Similar pairs of cases can be constructed for a variety of thoughts concerning artifactual and social kinds whose natures depend on intentions, conventions, laws, institutions, and the like that only a few members of society might know about.

Finally, a fourth line of reasoning targets normative and logical concepts and purports to establish their dependence on inferential dispositions.[21] I will focus on logical concepts.[22] Classical logic and intuitionist logic differ in what the valid rules of inference for the logical connectives are. Consider negation. In classical logic the following is valid: from "not not A" infer "A." In intuitionist logic it is not valid. One of the upshots of the differences between classical and intuitionist logic is that while in classical logic one can validly infer "if A, then B" from "if not B, then not A," in intuitionist logic this is not a valid inference. These differences seem to constitute a difference in meaning. "Not" in classical logic means something different from "not" in intuitionist logic precisely because it is governed by different rules of inference. So consider the following two cases:

Case 9: In the actual world, Clara has the inferential dispositions characteristic of classical logic and thinks something she expresses by saying,
"If this isn't funny, then I'm not sane."

Case 10: In a counterfactual scenario, Clara is in the same phenomenal
state but has the inferential dispositions characteristic of intuitionist logic
and thinks something she expresses by saying, "If this isn't funny, then
I'm not sane."

In Case 9, Clara has a thought from which she is disposed to infer that if
I'm sane, then this is funny. In Case 10, Clara has a thought from which
she is not disposed to infer that if I'm sane, then this is funny. So, it is
tempting to conclude, she has different thoughts even though she is in the
same phenomenal state. Notice that she might not be in the same brain state.
Plausibly, the differences in her dispositions depend on differences in her
brain. But here we have a case where the difference in brain state does not
make a phenomenal difference. The different inferential dispositions have
implications for what she would do were she to make an inference, but
they need not make any phenomenal difference at the time at which she
thinks the thoughts she expresses by saying, "If this isn't funny, then I'm
not sane."

Timothy Williamson has argued against the view that which logical concepts one deploys in thought depends on what one's inferential dispositions
are.[23] In elaborating his argument, however, Williamson appeals to the idea
that which logical concepts one deploys in thought depends on alternative
non-phenomenal factors, such as history and social environment. So even if
one is sympathetic with Williamson's reasoning, that reasoning does not
provide any support for the view that phenomenal states might determine
normative and logical concepts. Rather, it supports the view that normative
and logical concepts should be assimilated to natural and artifactual kinds.

Altogether, then, reflection on these cases lends support to the claim that
cognitive intentional states that involve demonstrative, indexical, nominal,
natural, mathematical, artifactual, social, normative, or logical concepts do
not constitutively depend on phenomenal states alone, which is premise
(2) in the argument against Cognitive Phenomenal Intentionality. Further,
it seems to me that the cases reinforce each other because together they
bring to light a general phenomenon that is only hinted at when they are
considered in isolation. The general phenomenon is that cognitive intentional
states do not seem intelligible in isolation, but only in a larger context that

includes the things we think about, their underlying natures, other people, and larger patterns in our cognitive activity.

Options

The previous two sections suggest that there is something of a paradox in how we represent our own phenomenally conscious cognitive intentional states in imagination. Take some phenomenally conscious cognitive intentional state, e.g. thinking that water is clear. One thing we might do is keep it in mind and imagine states with the same phenomenal character. When we do this, it seems that these phenomenally identical states will also be intentionally identical, or at least intentionally rather similar. This sort of reasoning suggests Cognitive Phenomenal Intentionality. Another thing we might do is focus on the phenomenal state associated with some occurrence of the thought that water is clear and imagine that phenomenal state occurring in different contexts – in the presence of different objects, underlying natures, societies, and inferential dispositions. When we do this, it seems that one and the same phenomenal state might be associated with the occurrence of phenomenally conscious cognitive states that are intentionally distinct, and even intentionally rather dissimilar. This sort of reasoning undermines Cognitive Phenomenal Intentionality.

In this section I will describe three options for responding to the tension between these two lines of reasoning without completely giving up on Cognitive Phenomenal Intentionality. They are: phenomenal externalism, content internalism, and partial determinism.

One possibility for resolving the tension is to adopt phenomenal externalism.[24] According to phenomenal internalism phenomenal states do not constitutively depend on factors such as objects present, underlying natures, societies, and inferential dispositions. According to phenomenal externalism phenomenal states do constitutively depend on one or another of these factors. If phenomenal externalism is true, then the argument against Cognitive Phenomenal Intentionality breaks down in its presentation of the cases. In each pair of cases I assumed there could be exact phenomenal similarity despite a difference in what objects are present, or what the underlying natures of some kinds are, or what social conventions are in place, or what one's inferential dispositions are. If phenomenal externalism is true, then this assumption is mistaken.

Phenomenal externalism remains unpopular among proponents of Cognitive Phenomenal Intentionality. What might be wrong with it? The main independent consideration against it derives from reflection on what we can imagine. It seems we can imagine phenomenal duplicates who are not duplicates with respect to the broad factors on which, according to phenomenal externalism, phenomenal states constitutively depend. One worry about this consideration is that the most well-developed examples focus on sensory phenomenal states.[25] It might be that sensory phenomenal states are narrow but cognitive phenomenal states are not. Another worry is that the argument from what we can imagine might be misleading. It might mislead us because our imagination is faulty. Or it might mislead us because our interpretation of what we imagine is mistaken. That is, we might imagine a genuinely possible scenario but mistakenly interpret it as one in which there are phenomenal duplicates.

There is little independent argument against phenomenal externalism in the literature on Cognitive Phenomenal Intentionality. The real explanation for its neglect, it seems to me, is that proponents of Cognitive Phenomenal Intentionality take it to be unmotivated. If there is a viable notion of narrow content, then phenomenal externalism is unmotivated. And by far the most popular strategy for resolving the tension between the arguments for and against Cognitive Phenomenal Intentionality is to endorse some form of content internalism.

So let us explore this strategy. The basic idea is that the two lines of reasoning are both correct but about different things – about different sorts of cognitive intentional state. There are narrow cognitive intentional states for which Cognitive Phenomenal Intentionality is true. And there are broad cognitive intentional states for which Cognitive Phenomenal Intentionality is false.

Some cognitive intentional states have contents that we routinely attribute using natural language "that" clauses. If the content is truth conditional, then we can attribute it using one such clause. We say: Oscar thinks that water is clear. If the content is of the sort that is more or less accurate rather than true or false, i.e. if it determines accuracy conditions rather than truth conditions, then we can attribute it using more than one "that" clause. Take the state of understanding an argument. Plausibly, this is not just true or false. It is more or less accurate depending on how good the understanding is. So we might say: Oscar is in a state of understanding part of whose content is that the conclusion of the argument is such and such, and part of whose content is that the premises of the argument are this and that, and part of whose content is that the premises support the conclusion thusly, and part of whose content is that the most controversial premise is this one, etc. Roughly, Oscar's state of understanding the argument is accurate to the degree that its truth-conditional parts are true.

Reflection on cognitive intentional states with contents that we routinely attribute using natural language "that" clauses suggests that they constitutively depend on broad factors – on factors such as objects present, underlying natures, society, and inferential dispositions. If there are narrow cognitive intentional states, then their contents will be different. Proponents of the content internalist strategy must explain what these narrow contents are.

Take Oscar and Twin Oscar. Speaking English, I say: Oscar thinks that water is clear. Speaking Twin English, I say: Oscar thinks that water is clear. The first claim attributes a thought that is true just in case H_2O is clear. The second claim attributes a thought that is true just in case XYZ is clear. These are broad cognitive intentional states. Oscar has the first, but not the second. Twin Oscar has the second, but not the first. According to the content internalist, there is another cognitive intentional state. It is one that Oscar and Twin Oscar share, and it is determined by their common phenomenal state. So one wants to know: What is this cognitive intentional state? What are its truth conditions? The literature contains resources for answering these questions in a number of different ways. I will consider three representative ideas: the first derives from Bertrand Russell and appeals to descriptions, the second derives from Gottlob Frege and appeals to modes of presentation, and the third derives from Rudolf Carnap and appeals to intensions.

In one phase of his thought, Bertrand Russell believed three claims that we might formulate as follows.[26] First, the contents of cognitive intentional states are complexes made out of their subject matter. So the content of the thought that water is clear is a complex made out of the substance water and the property of being clear. Second, one can be in a cognitive intentional state with a certain content only if one is acquainted with the constituents of that content. So one can think that water is clear only if one is acquainted with the substance water and with the property of being clear. Third, the only objects of one's acquaintance are one's self, one's sense data, and universals. So, return to the thought that water is clear. The substance water is neither my self, one of my sense data, nor a universal. So really I can't think that water is clear. If I think a thought that one might attribute to me using the clause, "that water is clear," what I am really thinking is something along the lines of what one might attribute using the clause, "that the watery stuff around me is clear." This thought's constituents are me, the property of being the watery stuff around me, and the property of being clear. Russell's three commitments imply that natural language attributions of cognitive intentional states are poor guides to their actual contents because they use terms for things other than selves, sense data, or universals. Their actual contents can be reported by replacing these terms with descriptions that specify those things solely in terms of how they relate to selves, sense data, and universals.

One way of developing the content internalist strategy is to pursue a project like the one that Russell's commitments suggest.[27] Broad cognitive intentional states have their contents routinely attributed using natural language "that" clauses. Narrow cognitive intentional states have contents that can be reported by replacing most of the terms in such "that" clauses with descriptions that specify their subject matter in terms that are available to all phenomenal duplicates. So the narrow cognitive intentional state Oscar and Twin Oscar share because of their common phenomenal state might be the thought that the watery stuff around me is clear.

The main worry about this strategy is that there might be no such descriptions.[28] If "watery stuff" means "stuff like water" then the concept it expresses is available to Oscar but not to Twin Oscar – taking my current usage of "water" to be in English not Twin English. So we need some other description. One might try "clear, drinkable, liquid that fills the lakes and oceans." But arguably all of these properties – being clear, being drinkable, being a liquid, filling lakes, and filling oceans – are natural kinds or at least like natural kinds in having underlying natures. One might try to formulate a description that only contains terms for phenomenal states. Maybe such a description for water can be found, though there is little reason to be confident that this is so. Even if one can be found, however, another problem remains. Whatever the description is, it will have a logical form, and as we saw above, there are reasons to doubt that cognitive intentional states that involve logical concepts constitutively depend on phenomenal states alone.

The second way of developing the internalist strategy derives from Frege.[29] Whereas Russell took the contents of cognitive intentional states to be made out of their subject matter – i.e. out of the objects and properties they are about – Frege took the contents of cognitive intentional states to be made out of modes of presentation of their subject matter – i.e. out of modes of presentation of the objects and properties they are about.[30] A mode of presentation of something is a way of representing that thing. Crucially, there can be more than one mode of presentation of the same thing: Mark Twain might be thought of as the author of *Huckleberry Finn* or as the author of *Adventures of Tom Sawyer*. These are different modes of presentation of one person.

To see the motivation for Frege's view about the contents of cognitive intentional states, consider the following two beliefs: the belief that Mark Twain is Mark Twain and the belief that Mark Twain is Samuel Clemens. These seem like different beliefs. One might have the first but lack the second if one didn't know that Mark Twain is indeed Samuel Clemens. The most natural answer to the question of what makes these beliefs different is that they have different contents. If we adopt a Russellian view about contents, however, then this answer is unavailable. Mark Twain is Samuel Clemens. So there is just the one person. If "Mark Twain is Mark Twain" and "Mark Twain is Samuel Clemens" express contents whose constituents are the objects and properties they are about, then they pick out the same content. At least this is so on a naively Russellian view that does not replace "Mark Twain" and "Samuel Clemens" with descriptions. The Fregean view does not face this problem. According to the Fregean view the contents are different because their constituents are modes of presentation and the mode of presentation associated with "Mark Twain" is different from the mode of presentation associated with "Samuel Clemens."

Nothing I have said so far indicates how modes of presentation might help in developing the content internalist strategy. From what I have said so far we can see how modes of presentation enable us to distinguish between cognitive intentional states that are about the same things. What we are looking for, however, is a way of identifying cognitive intentional states that are about different things. So we must make another assumption about modes of presentation. We must assume that one and the same mode of presentation might be a mode of presentation of different things in different contexts. Take, for example, the mode of presentation of Mark Twain associated with thinking of him as the author of *Huckleberry Finn*. According to the understanding of modes of presentation required for present purposes, that very mode of presentation would have been a mode of presentation of a different person had someone else written *Huckleberry Finn*.[31]

Now let us return to Oscar and Twin Oscar. If we think of their cognitive intentional states along naively Russellian lines, then they must be different: Oscar's thought contains H_2O as a constituent; Twin Oscar's thought contains XYZ as a constituent. The basic idea behind the Fregean approach to developing the internalist strategy is to argue that even if there are these distinct Russellian cognitive intentional states, there is also a common Fregean cognitive intentional state, which cognitive intentional state is determined by Oscar and Twin Oscar's common phenomenal state. The common Fregean cognitive intentional state will have as a constituent a common mode of presentation that is a mode of presentation of H_2O when it occurs in Earth-bound thoughts and that is a mode of presentation of XYZ when it occurs in Twin Earth-bound thoughts. The same idea might be applied to the other cases we considered in the previous section. When Oscar and Twin Oscar think thoughts they give expression to using the term "curve," for example, their thoughts refer to different mathematical kinds, but they might do so via the same mode of presentation.

The main worry about this strategy is that it is not really clear what these modes of presentation are supposed to be. When I introduced the idea of a mode of presentation I used descriptions. "The author of *Huckleberry Finn*" picks out a mode of presentation of Mark Twain. If we ask what is the mode of presentation that Oscar and Twin Oscar deploy in the Fregean cognitive intentional states they express using the term "water" we might say it is picked out by "the watery stuff around me." And if we ask what is the mode of presentation that Oscar and Twin Oscar deploy in the Fregean cognitive intentional states they express using the term "curve" we might say it is picked out by "the kind of figure that results from deforming a line."

So one idea about modes of presentation is this: a mode of presentation is a complex made out of the objects and properties referred to in a corresponding description. If this is what modes of presentation are, however, then the Fregean strategy under consideration does not have any advantages over the descriptivist strategy considered above. It has advantages over a naive Russellian view. But it does not have any advantages over a descriptivist Russellian view.

Another idea about modes of presentation is this: a mode of presentation is a condition expressed by a corresponding description. This is a different view because two descriptions referring to different objects and properties can express the same condition. Consider, for example, the descriptions "the stuff superficially like H_2O" and "the stuff superficially like XYZ." These make reference to different things, but arguably they express the same condition since stuff is superficially like H_2O in the relevant sense just in case it is superficially like XYZ in the relevant sense. So while only Oscar can be in cognitive intentional states whose contents contain H_2O as a constituent, both Oscar and Twin Oscar can be in cognitive intentional states whose contents contain the condition of being the stuff superficially like H_2O as a constitution. We refer to H_2O in order to pick out the condition. But one might just as well refer to XYZ in order to pick out the condition. How one picks out the condition is one thing. What the condition is in itself is another: the condition has its own identity independent of the ways we have of picking it out.

That said, one still wants to know what this identity is. There are various questions that arise about modes of presentation: What modes of presentation are there? When is a mode of presentation available to a thinker and why? How do modes of presentation determine referents and truth and accuracy conditions given a context? Without some account of the identities of modes of presentation it is difficult to see how to give principled answers to these questions. But these are precisely the questions for which we need principled answers if we are to assess the plausibility of Cognitive Phenomenal Intentionality.

Enter intensions. The third way of developing the internalist strategy can be seen as an attempt to say what modes of presentation are. The basic idea is that they are intensions. The current understanding of this notion derives from Carnap.[32] We can explain it in terms of two other notions. First, there is the space of possible worlds. There are different maximally specific ways the world could be. Each such way is a possible world. And all together they form the space of possible worlds. Second, there is the extension of a concept or thought relative to a possible world. Take the concept of being an author. In the actual world this concept applies to a certain set of individuals. This set is its extension relative to the actual world. In some other possible world different individuals will be authors. The extension of the concept of being an author relative to that possible world will be a different set of individuals. Similarly, take the thought that Mark Twain is an author. In the actual world this thought is true. The truth-value Truth is its extension relative to the actual world. In some other possible world Mark Twain is not an author. The extension of the thought that Mark Twain is an author relative to that possible world will be the truth-value False. The intension associated with a concept or thought is just a function that encodes information about its extension relative to each possible world: it is a function from the space of possible worlds to extensions.

Consider, then, Oscar's thought that water is clear. The intension associated with Oscar's concept of being clear is a function that takes a possible world as input and returns the clear things there as output. Given the actual world as input, it returns a set containing water among other things as output. Given some other possible world as input, it might return some different set as output. The intension associated with Oscar's concept for water is a function that takes a possible world as input and returns the water there as output. Given the actual world as input, it returns H_2O as output. Given some other possible world as input, might it return something other than H_2O as output? In this case, plausibly the answer is no. There is a difference between the concept of water and the concept of being clear. Clear things might not have been clear and unclear things might have been clear. But water, it seems, is necessarily H_2O. Its chemical composition is its underlying nature and underlying natures are essential.[33] The intension associated with Oscar's whole thought that water is clear, then, will be true relative to a possible world w just in case H_2O is clear in w.

The upshot of the foregoing is that intensions do not automatically provide us with the resources to explain what the contents of narrow cognitive intentional states might be. The thought Oscar expresses when he says, "water is clear," is true relative to a possible world w just in case H_2O is clear in w. The thought Twin Oscar expresses when he says, "water is clear," is true relative to a possible world w just in case XYZ is clear in w. These are different intensions. So if the contents of their thoughts are these intensions, then their thoughts are different. We have not found some cognitive intentional state common to both Oscar and Twin Oscar.

There are different ways of elaborating on the appeal to intensions so that it might better serve the content internalist's purposes. David Chalmers has pursued this project most thoroughly.[34] The basic observation motivating his approach is that even though it is necessary that water is H_2O it is not a priori knowable that water is H_2O. You can't tell that water is H_2O just by thinking really hard about water. Rather, you have to go out and make some observations. Since it is necessary that water is H_2O, there is no maximally specific way the world could be in which water is not H_2O. That is, there is no possible world in which water is not H_2O. Since it is not a priori that water is H_2O, however, there is a maximally specific way the world might be, for all we can tell a priori, in which water is not H_2O. If you consider maximally specific descriptions of how the world might be and you allow anything to go into one of these descriptions so long as it can't be ruled out a priori and it is consistent with everything else in the description, then there will be such a description according to which water is not H_2O. One example would be a description according to which water is XYZ. That is not a genuine possibility, but it is also not something we can rule out a priori. Chalmers calls maximally specific ways the world might be, for all we can tell a priori, epistemically possible scenarios, or just scenarios for short. So even though there is no possible world in which water is not H_2O, there is an epistemically possible scenario in which water is not H_2O, in which, say, it is XYZ instead.

Epistemically possible scenarios are different from but analogous to possible worlds. This suggests a construction that parallels the construction of intensions but replaces possible worlds with scenarios. Chalmers calls the results of the new construction primary or epistemic intensions. In outline, and setting aside lots of subtleties that will not matter for our purposes, the construction goes like this. First, there is the space of scenarios. These are different maximally specific ways the world might be for all we can tell a priori. Second, given any scenario and any thought, there is a procedure for assigning that thought a truth-value relative to that scenario: you suppose that the scenario is how things actually turn out to be, and you reason about whether the thought turns out to be true on that hypothesis. Take the thought that water is H_2O. And consider the scenario in which H_2O is the watery stuff. If this scenario is how things actually turn out to be, then water is H_2O. So the thought that water is H_2O is true relative to this scenario. Now consider the scenario in which XYZ is the watery stuff. If this scenario is how things actually turn out to be, then water is not H_2O – it is XYZ instead. So the thought that water is H_2O is false relative to this scenario. This is different from the result we would have got if we took for granted that water is actually H_2O and considered these scenarios as counterfactual scenarios. If we adopted that procedure, then the thought that water is H_2O would come out true relative to both scenarios. With respect to the scenario in which XYZ is the watery stuff we would say that something other than water, namely XYZ, is the watery stuff. The epistemic intension associated with a thought is a function that encodes the results of Chalmers's alternative procedure: it is a function from the space of scenarios to truth-values – where these truth-values are determined by the procedure of considering scenarios as hypotheses about the actual world rather than as counterfactuals.

Let us return to Oscar's thought that water is clear. The standard intension associated with Oscar's thought is a function from possible worlds to truth-values such that Oscar's thought is true relative to a possible world w just in case H_2O is clear in w. The epistemic intension associated with Oscar's thought is a function from scenarios to truth-values such that Oscar's thought is true relative to a scenario s just in case the watery stuff is clear in s. If in s the watery stuff is XYZ and XYZ but not H_2O is clear, still Oscar's thought comes out true in s because then, as we saw above, in s water is XYZ. Now consider the thought Twin Oscar expresses by saying, "water is clear." The standard intension associated with Twin Oscar's thought is a function from possible worlds to truth-values such that Twin Oscar's thought is true relative to a possible world w just in case XYZ is clear in w. The epistemic intension associated with Oscar's thought is a function from scenarios to truth-values such that Twin Oscar's thought is true relative to a scenario s just in case the watery stuff is clear in s. If in s the watery stuff is H_2O and H_2O but not XYZ is clear, still Twin Oscar's thought comes out true in s because then, as we saw above, in s water is H_2O. So even though Oscar and Twin Oscar think thoughts associated with different standard intensions, they think thoughts associated with the same epistemic intension. The content internalist can identify the common cognitive intentional state with the state of thinking a thought associated with the common epistemic intension.

What follows about the prospects of Cognitive Phenomenal Intentionality? I will briefly indicate three reasons for curbing one's optimism.

First, one might worry about the general construction of epistemic intensions. There must be a semantically neutral language for describing scenarios. Roughly, the semantic properties of a semantically neutral language do not depend on broad factors. It contains terms that work the way we have been pretending the term "watery stuff" works rather than the way terms such as "water" work. And given any scenario described in this language and any thought, there must be an a priori answer to the question of whether the thought is true on the hypothesis that the scenario is actual. Whether there is such a language for which there are such a priori answers is controversial.[35]

Second, the construction of epistemic intensions might not really provide a good account of modes of presentation. Consider these two beliefs: the belief that curves are curves; the belief that curves are continuous mappings of the unit interval. These seem like different beliefs. One might have the first but lack the second if one didn't know that curves are continuous mappings of the unit interval. The most natural answer to the question of what makes these beliefs different is that they have different contents. This is just the same line of reasoning we took when considering the belief that Mark Twain is Mark Twain and the belief that Mark Twain is Samuel Clemens. If modes of presentation distinguish the two beliefs about the author, then they should also distinguish the two beliefs about the mathematical kind. But these two beliefs are associated with the same epistemic intension. The reason is that it is a priori that curves are continuous mappings of the unit interval. Both the beliefs that curves are curves and the belief that curves are continuous mappings of the unit interval are associated with the epistemic intension that returns the truth-value Truth given any epistemically possible scenario as input. This casts doubt on the idea that modes of presentation should be identified with epistemic intensions.[36]

Third, the epistemic intension associated with a thought might not depend on its phenomenal character alone. Epistemic intensions are neutral between some broad factors. But that does not show that they depend on phenomenal character alone. Maybe they also depend on dispositions. Why is Oscar's thought that water is clear true relative to a scenario s just in case the watery stuff is clear in s? One answer is that it is at least in part because Oscar – or Oscar suitably idealized – has dispositions to make judgments according to which the thought that water is clear is true relative to a scenario s just in case the watery stuff is clear in s. Had Oscar's dispositions been different, then the epistemic intension associated with Oscar's thought would have been different. But as we saw when considering logical concepts, sameness of phenomenal states does not guarantee sameness of dispositions. This remains true even if we consider phenomenal states over time. Suppose Oscar and Twin Oscar are phenomenal duplicates throughout their lives. There will be some judgments they are never called on to make. And Oscar and Twin Oscar might have different dispositions with respect to these judgments.

Let us turn to another option for resolving the tensions between the arguments for and against Cognitive Phenomenal Intentionality. This option is to qualify the Cognitive Phenomenal Intentionality thesis so that it is about partial rather than full determination – i.e. adopt what I call partial determinism. Maybe phenomenal states play some role in determining cognitive intentional states, but they cannot get the job done without some help from broad, non-phenomenal factors. If this is the correct view then the argument for Cognitive Phenomenal Intentionality is misleading. It suggests a phenomenal state is enough for an intentional state. But this is not so. Perhaps we are misled because when we have a cognitive state in mind and we imagine a phenomenal duplicate of that state, we also implicitly imagine some of the necessary broad, non-phenomenal factors to be present as well.

I believe this sort of view requires understanding the determination relation to be a matter of grounding rather than necessitation. Necessitation is all or nothing: a phenomenal state implies a cognitive intentional state or it doesn't. One might say that a phenomenal state partially implies a cognitive intentional state just in case it plus some supplementation jointly imply the cognitive intentional state. But this idea is not discriminating enough. One could say the same thing about any other state that has nothing to do with intentionality or even anything to do with the mind. Grounding is different. If a car is parked next to a fire hydrant, then it makes sense to say that that fact partly grounds the fact that the car is illegally parked. It is only a partial ground because the full ground depends on the laws about parking. But it is at least a partial ground because the fact that the car is parked next to a fire hydrant is explanatorily relevant to the fact that the car is illegally parked. Grounding can be partial precisely because it is an explanatory relation and so there is a notion of explanatory relevance that applies to it.

We already observed some difficulties with the idea that phenomenal states ground cognitive intentional states. Here I think they are exacerbated. If we suppose some phenomenal states ground cognitive intentional states, then that raises the question of what the phenomenal states themselves are. Earlier we considered the prospects of combining the grounding view with the view that they are identical to cognitive intentional states. That option is ruled out here. For if phenomenal states were identical to cognitive intentional states, then they would necessitate cognitive intentional states. But we are now operating under the assumption that phenomenal states do not necessitate cognitive intentional states, that they require supplementation from some broad, non-phenomenal factors.

One option is to argue that the phenomenal states that partly ground cognitive intentional states are cognitive "raw feels" or cognitive "non-intentional qualia."[37] They are feels or qualia because they are phenomenal states. They are cognitive because wholly sensory states do not suffice for them. And they are raw or non-intentional because they are not themselves intentional states, they do not have intentional content. If there are such states, that might be surprising. But I do not think it would be outlandish. They would be the cognitive version of something many writers believe exist in the case of sensory experience.[38] And the fact that we do not observe such cognitive raw feels is not evidence that they do not exist. Cognitive raw feels are phenomenal state types. Whenever such a type is tokened, however, plausibly the token is one or another phenomenally conscious cognitive intentional state with a specific content. That is because every such token will occur in a context that includes the assortment of non-phenomenal factors required to fully determine that content. So we never find token mental states that are mere cognitive raw feels to pick out and contemplate.

The main problem with this option, it seems to me, is that it faces a dilemma. Either it is part of the nature of cognitive raw feels to place some constraints on content, or it is not. Consider the first option. Maybe when Oscar and Twin Oscar each think the thought they express by saying "water is clear" they share a cognitive raw feel that constrains them to be consciously predicating clarity of some watery natural kind or other. The worry about this option is that it is difficult to see how to spell it out in detail without recourse to some notion of narrow content. It looks as if the shared cognitive raw feel is not really non-intentional; rather it is a narrow cognitive intentional state representing that the watery stuff, whatever natural kind that turns out to be, is clear.[39] Consider, then, the second option. Maybe when Oscar and Twin Oscar each think the thought they express by saying "water is clear" they share a cognitive raw feel that we pick out as the phenomenal state that thinkers have in common when they consciously predicate clarity of some watery natural kind. This is just our way of picking the phenomenal state out. But the phenomenal state's nature is independent of how we pick it out.[40] So even if we pick the phenomenal state out by its relation to intentional states, the phenomenal state itself might not be in any sense intentional. The worry about this option is that it is difficult to see why such a phenomenal state should play any role in grounding cognitive intentional states. Maybe such a cognitive raw feel exists. But what contribution it might make in grounding cognitive intentional states remains a mystery.

Notes

1 See Quine 1960.
2 See Kripke 1982.
3 See how Fodor 1987 puts it.
4 This idea can be found in Searle 1987, Horgan and Graham 2012, and Strawson 2011.
5 See Jenkins 2011 and Kriegel 2013.
6 Kriegel's (2011) view seems to have this structure.
7 See, for example, Boghossian 1989 and McDowell 1981, 1984.
8 Bayne 2009, 22, as reprinted in Hawley and Macpherson 2011.
9 Brogaard 2013, 39.
10 See ibid.
11 Siewert 1998, 221.
12 See Siewert 1998 and Horgan and Tienson 2002.
13 Ibid., 527, in Chalmers 2002b.
14 See their endnote 23.
15 See, for example, Lakatos 1976.
16 John McDowell has forcefully defended and elaborated this kind of argument in a number of works collected in McDowell 1998. See also Burge 1977, Evans 1982, and Kripke 1980.
17 See Putnam 1975, Burge 1979, Kripke 1980.

18 Putnam 1975.
19 This line of reasoning is most associated with the work of Burge. See the essays in Burge 2007.
20 See Burge 1979.
21 See Sellars 1954, Block 1986, Brandom 1994.
22 See McDowell 1979 for one way of drawing the connection to normative concepts.
23 See Williamson 2007.
24 See Harman 1990, Tye 1995, Lycan 1996.
25 See, for example, Block 1990.
26 See Russell 1903, 1905, 1910, 1912.
27 For versions of this strategy see Searle 1983 and Mendola 2008.
28 See LePore and Loewer 1986.
29 It is developed with respect to perceptual phenomenal intentionality in Chalmers 2006a and Thompson 2010.
30 See Frege 1948, 1956.
31 The assumption is controversial. Some proponents of Fregean ideas about content deny it. See, for example, Evans 1982 and the papers in McDowell 1998.
32 See Carnap 1947.
33 See Kripke 1980.
34 See, especially, Chalmers 2006b, 2012.
35 For some criticisms see Byrne and Pryor 2006, Block and Stalnaker 1999, Schroeter 2014, Neta 2014. Chalmers replies to the earlier criticisms in Chalmers 2012 and to Schroeter and Neta in Chalmers 2014.
36 For an elaboration of this sort of worry see Stanley 2014. Chalmers replies in Chalmers 2014.
37 I think something like this view might be found in Husserl 1997, 1982, and maybe Loar 2003 and Strawson 2011.
38 See, for example, Husserl 1997, Block 1990, 2003, and Peacocke 1983.
39 Perhaps some of the technical devices worked out in the literature on relativist semantics will provide resources for developing a significantly different alternative to standard content internalism. See MacFarlane 2005 for an introduction to relativist semantics, and see Brogaard 2010, 2012 and Farkas 2008a, 2008b for potential applications to phenomenal intentionality.
40 For an illuminating discussion of this sort of point and an application of it to puzzles about perceptual experience see Nida-Rümelin 2011.

Further reading

See Montague (2010) for a helpful survey of both the background to and the literature on phenomenal intentionality in general and cognitive phenomenal intentionality in particular. Block (1990), Harman (1990), Siewert (1998), Horgan and Tienson (2002), and Loar (2003) are early discussions that lay out many of the basic issues. Pitt (2009), Strawson (2011), and Kriegel (2011) represent different takes on how to carry out what Kriegel calls the phenomenal intentionality research program. Chalmers (2004) is a helpful survey of different ways of thinking about phenomenal content.

CONCLUSION

Let's take stock. In the introduction, I distinguished four theses:

Phenomenal Presence: Some cognitive states put one in phenomenal states.

Irreducibility: Some cognitive states put one in phenomenal states for which no wholly sensory states suffice.

Independence: Some cognitive states put one in phenomenal states that are independent of sensory states.

Cognitive Phenomenal Intentionality: Some phenomenal states determine cognitive intentional states.

Phenomenal Presence should be common ground: everyone can agree that some cognition is phenomenally conscious even if there are disagreements about the nature of the phenomenal states involved in it.

I see Irreducibility as the main point of dispute between proponents and opponents of cognitive phenomenology. The arguments in favor of it include introspective arguments, inferences to the best explanation of certain forms of self-knowledge, phenomenal contrast arguments, and arguments from value. Though I think some of these arguments are inconclusive, some unsound, and some dialectically weak, overall I think the case in favor of Irreducibility is very strong and that it should be accepted. The main arguments against it include introspective arguments, arguments from the temporal structure of thought, and arguments to the effect that it is entangled with the third thesis, Independence. I do not think any of these arguments holds up under scrutiny.

Independence and Cognitive Phenomenal Intentionality are stronger than Irreducibility in that they imply Irreducibility but Irreducibility does not imply them. Independence is questionable on phenomenal holist grounds. The status of Cognitive Phenomenal Intentionality seems to me to be an open question.

What about the significance of cognitive phenomenology? In the introduction, I distinguished three areas to which cognitive phenomenology might be relevant: epistemology, value theory, and semantics. But that was before getting into exactly what commitment to cognitive phenomenology amounts to. Now that we have isolated Irreducibility as the main issue and clarified its content by exploring various arguments for and against it, it is worth reconsidering what all the fuss might be about.

I will conclude by sketching one line of reasoning in favor of thinking that cognitive phenomenology is significant for epistemology, value theory, and semantics. The idea is that phenomenology in general is connected to these areas via the notion of awareness, and cognitive phenomenology in particular is connected to them via the notion of awareness of abstract reality.

Awareness, recall, is a two-place determinable relation between a subject and an object. Examples include: seeing a flat-tailed horned lizard, hearing a bird chirp, and feeling a mosquito bite. In each case, you are aware of something in part because it is phenomenally differentiated from some background. Take the flat-tailed horned lizard. If the flat-tailed horned lizard is camouflaged against the sand, then even though it is there and it is a direct partial cause of whatever phenomenal state you are in, you are not visually aware of it. So there is a connection between awareness and phenomenology. The connection is the one that camouflage exploits: camouflage blocks awareness by preventing this necessary phenomenal condition on awareness from obtaining.

Suppose it is not camouflaged and you are visually aware of the flat-tailed horned lizard. Plausibly, because you are aware of it, three things follow. First, you can pick the lizard out in demonstrative thoughts. That is, you can entertain thoughts you might report by saying, "That is a flat-tailed horned lizard," and the demonstrative concept expressed in your use of "that" will refer to the lizard you see. This is a connection between awareness and semantics. Second, you will be in a position to make judgments about the lizard. Suppose you wonder whether there is a lizard nearby. You just don't know. Then you see the flat-tailed horned lizard. Now you do know. Because you see the flat-tailed horned lizard, you know that there is a lizard nearby. This is a connection between awareness and epistemology. Third, you will be able to contemplate the lizard as an object of aesthetic appreciation. Suppose I tell you about the wonders of flat-tailed horned lizards, but you never see one for yourself. Then you are informed about the wonders of flat-tailed horned lizards, but you do not experience these for yourself. Visual awareness of the flat-tailed horned lizard makes the difference. And insofar as experiencing wonders is a good thing, there is this connection between awareness and value theory.

The foregoing suggests that sensory phenomenology is essential to at least some thought, knowledge, and appreciation of concrete things because of its connection to sensory awareness. Plausibly, the same pattern exists in the case of cognition: cognitive phenomenology is essential to at least some thought, knowledge, and appreciation of abstract things via its connection to intellectual awareness.

Consider the following from Husserl:

> A memorial consciousness – for example, of a landscape – is not originarily presentive; the landscape is not perceived as it would be in case we actually saw it. By this we do not mean to say that memorial consciousness has no competence of its own; only that it is not a "seeing" consciousness. Phenomenology brings to light an analogue of this contrast in *each of the other kinds of positing* mental processes. For example: We can assert "blindly" that two plus one is equal to one plus two; but we can also make this same judgment in the manner peculiar to intellectual seeing. When we do this, the predicatively formed affair-complex, the synthetical objectivity corresponding to the judgment-synthesis, is given originarily, seized upon in an originary manner.[1]

Husserl makes two contrasts: perception contrasts with memory; and intuition – "intellectual seeing" – contrasts with blind judgment. I might recall a landscape. I might think demonstrative thoughts about it, go over what I know about it, and appreciate its beauties. But my capacity to do these things depends on a prior perception of the landscape: it was a previous sensory awareness that enabled the demonstrative thoughts, gave me the knowledge, and put me in a position to appreciate. This is what makes perception "originary." According to Husserl, there is a similar relationship between intuition and thoughts, knowledge, and appreciation of abstract truths such as the truth that $2 + 1 = 1 + 2$ or the more general truth that addition is commutative. Suppose someone tells me that addition is commutative, but I do not "see" it for myself. Then I might very well believe that addition is commutative. But this would be judging blindly. Suppose, however, I do "see" it for myself. What does this consist in? According to Husserl it consists in seizing on the relevant "affair-complex." What that means is that it consists in being aware of the state of affairs that addition is commutative. This is not sensory awareness. It is intellectual awareness. And just as with sensory awareness, intellectual awareness is "originary": it is a ground of demonstrative thought, knowledge, and the position to appreciate. In this case, the objects of such thought, knowledge, and appreciation are abstract rather than concrete.

Some of the examples we considered in previous chapters support Husserl's view. In chapter 2, we considered the case of intuiting: you intuit that if $a < 1$, then $2 - 2a > 0$ and in doing so you seem to be aware of the relevant "affair-complex" i.e. of how a's being less than 1 makes $2a$ smaller than 2 and so $2 - 2a$ greater than 0. In chapter 3, we considered the case of appreciating the charm of the proof that $(a + b)^2 \geq 4ab$. As with all aesthetic appreciation this depends on awareness, or at least seeming awareness, of the proof. We did not consider a case in which awareness of abstract objects grounds demonstrative thought. But it is easy to develop one on the basis of the cases already considered. Suppose I say to you, "There is this charming proof that $(a + b)^2 \geq 4ab$," and you reply, "I'd like to see it." You are able to think about the proof without standing in the intellectual awareness to it. But this ability depends on my report. Suppose you are aware of the proof. Then this awareness will give you the ability to think a thought you might express by saying, "That proof is charming," and your use of "that" corresponds to a capacity to entertain demonstrative thoughts about the proof that does not depend on anyone's report, but just on your awareness of the proof.

If these Husserlian thoughts about intellectual awareness are correct, then cognitive phenomenology is significant for epistemology, value theory, and semantics. Intellectual awareness, like any kind of awareness, is connected to phenomenology: the objects of intellectual awareness must not be camouflaged. We tend not to use the term "camouflage" here and it sounds odd. Perhaps there are better terms for the intellectual analogue, such as "obscurity" and "confusion." The terminology does not matter however. What is important is that just as with sensory awareness, intellectual awareness has necessary phenomenological conditions. The objects of intellectual awareness must phenomenally stand out from rather than blend into a cognitive background. In this case, however, it is implausible that the relevant phenomenology is sensory, or, rather, wholly sensory. It is clear how visual phenomenology might be so structured that in it a lizard stands out from sand and foliage. But it is not clear how visual phenomenology might be so structured that in it addition or commutativity stand out from other operations and properties such as multiplication and associativity. For that it looks like we need cognitive phenomenology.

Note

1 Husserl 1982, 326–327.

GLOSSARY

a priori justification A priori justification is traditionally taken to be justification that is independent of experience – where "experience" is assumed to be sensory.

awareness Objects of awareness are available to be picked out demonstratively because of how they are phenomenally differentiated from a background.

Cognitive Phenomenal Intentionality The thesis that some phenomenal states determine cognitive intentional states.

cognitive phenomenal state A phenomenal state for which wholly sensory states do not suffice.

cognitive state A partly cognitive state is one that represents part of its content in a cognitive way and a wholly cognitive state is one that represents all of its content in a cognitive way.

cognitive ways of representing Ways of representing that are independent of current awareness of environmental witnesses or states akin to such awareness.

conscious thought in the narrow sense A conscious cognitive state with the structure of a propositional attitude.

environmental witness An environmental witness to a proposition is something in a spatiotemporal region that either makes it true or indicates that it is true.

epistemic externalism Epistemic externalists deny that facts about what one is justified in believing are determined by facts one is in a position to ascertain by reflection alone – i.e. by introspection and a priori reasoning.

epistemic intension A function that encodes how a thought's truth-value varies when assessed relative to different suppositions about what scenario turns out to be actual.

epistemic internalism Epistemic internalists assert that facts about what one is justified in believing are determined by facts one is in a position to ascertain by reflection alone – i.e. by introspection and a priori reasoning.

extension The extension of a thought is its truth-value; the extensions of a thought's constituents (e.g. nominal and predicative concepts) are items that help to determine that thought's truth-value, e.g. individuals for nominal concepts and sets for predicative concepts.

final value The value something has for its own sake.

fitting attitude theories of value Theories that define having value in terms of being the object of a fitting evaluative attitude.

Fregean content Content made out of modes of presentation of the objects and properties that are its subject matter.

Gestaltism This is the idea that some partial phenomenal states depend on the whole phenomenal state to which they belong.

grounding The "in virtue of" relation invoked in non-causal explanations, often picked out by "because."

high-level perceptual content Perceptual content that goes beyond color, shape, pitch, etc., in that it represents features such as semantic properties, artifactual kinds, natural kinds, and causal relations.

Independence The thesis that some cognitive states put one in phenomenal states that are independent of sensory states.

instrumental value The value something has as a means to something else.

intension A function that encodes how a thought's truth-value varies when assessed relative to different possible worlds.

intentional content The sort of thing we characterize using "that" clauses and that is evaluable as true or false, or more or less accurate, relative to different ways the world could be.

intentional state A mental state that essentially has a certain intentional content.

Irreducibility The thesis that some cognitive states put one in phenomenal states for which wholly sensory states do not suffice.

low-level perceptual content Perceptual content that remains confined to color, shape, pitch, etc., and excludes features such as semantic properties, artifactual kinds, natural kinds, and causal relations.

mode of presentation A way of representing an object or property.

negative conceivability A state of affairs is negatively conceivable when it not a priori incoherent.

partial zombie A creature that is a functional duplicate of a normal human being but that lacks phenomenal states within a certain range – e.g. in a certain sensory modality.

phenomenal event or state A mental event or state individuated by its phenomenal character.

Phenomenal Holism This is the idea that all the partial phenomenal states in a total phenomenal state depend on that total phenomenal state.

Phenomenal Intentionality The thesis that some phenomenal states determine intentional states.

Phenomenal Presence The thesis that some cognitive states put one in phenomenal states.

phenomenal value Value possessed in virtue of phenomenology.

phenomenally conscious event or state A mental event or state that has a phenomenal character whenever it occurs, though this might differ on different occasions.

positive conceivability A state of affairs is positively conceivable when you can imagine a situation in which it obtains.

possible world A maximally specific way the world could be.

proposition The sort of thing picked out using a "that" clause and that is evaluable as true or false relative to different ways the world could be.

propositional attitude A mental state that consists of bearing an attitude – paradigmatically believing or desiring – to a proposition.

purely cognitive phenomenal state A phenomenal state for which wholly cognitive states suffice.

rational regret Regret it is rational to have about foregoing an option even if one pursued a better option.

Russellian content Content made out of the objects and properties that are its subject matter.

scenario A maximally specific way the world could be, for all we can tell a priori.

sensory phenomenal state A phenomenal state for which wholly sensory states suffice.

sensory state A partly sensory state is one that represents part of its content in a sensory way and a wholly sensory state is one that represents all of its content in a sensory way.

sensory ways of representing Ways of representing that are dependent on current awareness of environmental witnesses or states akin to such awareness.

transparency The idea that when one attends to a phenomenally conscious state the object of one's attention is the object presented in that state not the state itself.

vehicle of thought A sensible item that expresses the content of a thought.

Vehicle Proxy The thesis that if a conscious thought makes a phenomenal difference to one's overall experience, then it does so just because of the sensory appearance of a vehicle for that thought.

zombie A creature that is a functional duplicate of a normal human being but that lacks phenomenal states.

BIBLIOGRAPHY

Anderson, Elizabeth (1997) "Practical Reason and Incommensurable Goods,"
    in Ruth Chang (ed.), *Incommensurability, Incomparability and Practical
    Reason*, Cambridge, MA: Harvard University Press, 90–109.

Armstrong, David M. (1968) *A Materialist Theory of the Mind*, London:
    Routledge.

Bayne, Timothy J. (2009) "Perception and the Reach of Phenomenal Content,"
    Philosophical Quarterly 59 (236): 385–404.

——(2010) *The Unity of Consciousness*, Oxford: Oxford University Press.

Bayne, Timothy J., and Maja Spener (2010) "Introspective Humility," *Philosophical
    Issues* 20 (1): 1.

Bayne, Timothy J., and David J. Chalmers (2003) "What Is the Unity of Con-
    sciousness?" in Axel Cleeremans (ed.), *The Unity of Consciousness*,
    Oxford: Oxford University Press.

Bayne, Timothy J., and Michelle Montague (2011) "Cognitive Phenomenology:
    An Introduction," in Tim Bayne and Michelle Montague (eds.), *Cognitive
    Phenomenology*, Oxford: Oxford University Press, 2–34.

Beck, Jacob (2012) "The Generality Constraint and the Structure of Thought,"
    Mind 121 (483): 563–600.

Block, Ned (1986) "Advertisement for a Semantics for Psychology," *Midwest
    Studies in Philosophy* 10 (1): 615–678.

——(1990) "Inverted Earth," *Philosophical Perspectives* 4: 53–79.

——(2003) "Mental Paint," in Martin Hahn and B. Ramberg (eds.), *Reflections and Replies: Essays on the Philosophy of Tyler Burge*, Cambridge, MA: MIT Press, 165–200.

Block, Ned, and Robert Stalnaker (1999) "Conceptual Analysis, Dualism, and the Explanatory Gap," *Philosophical Review* 108 (1): 1–46.

Boghossian, Paul A. (1989) "The Rule-Following Considerations," *Mind* 98 (392): 507–549.

Brandom, Robert B. (1994) *Making It Explicit: Reasoning, Representing, and Discursive Commitment*, Cambridge, MA: Harvard University Press.

Brogaard, Berit (2010) "Strong Representationalism and Centered Content," *Philosophical Studies* 151 (3): 373–392.

——(2012) *Transient Truths: An Essay in the Metaphysics of Propositions*, Oxford: Oxford University Press.

——(2013) "Do We Perceive Natural Kind Properties?" *Philosophical Studies* 162 (1): 35–42.

Budd, Malcolm (2003) "The Acquaintance Principle," *British Journal of Aesthetics* 43 (4): 386–392.

Burge, Tyler (1977) "Belief De Re," *Journal of Philosophy* 74 (6): 338–362.

——(1979) "Individualism and the Mental," *Midwest Studies in Philosophy* 4 (1): 73–122.

——(2007) *Foundations of Mind*, Oxford: Oxford University Press.

Burton, Robert Alan (2008) *On Being Certain: Believing You Are Right Even When You're Not*, New York: St. Martin's Press

Byrne, Alex, and James Pryor (2006) "Bad Intensions," in Manuel Garcia-Carpintero and Josep Macià (eds.), *Two-Dimensional Semantics: Foundations and Applications*, Oxford: Oxford University Press, 38–54.

Carnap, Rudolf (1947) *Meaning and Necessity*, Chicago: University of Chicago Press.

Carruthers, Peter, and Bénédicte Veillet (2011) "The Case against Cognitive Phenomenology," in Tim Bayne and Michelle Montague (eds.), *Cognitive Phenomenology*, Oxford: Oxford University Press, 35–56.

Chalmers, David J. (1996) *The Conscious Mind: In Search of a Fundamental Theory*, Oxford: Oxford University Press.

——(2002a) "Does Conceivability Entail Possibility?" in Tamar S. Gendler and John Hawthorne (eds.), *Conceivability and Possibility*, Oxford: Oxford University Press, 145–200.

——(ed.) (2002b) *Philosophy of Mind: Classical and Contemporary Readings*, Oxford: Oxford University Press.

——(2004) "The Representational Character of Experience," in Brian Leiter (ed.), *The Future for Philosophy*, Oxford: Oxford University Press, 153–181.

——(2006a) "Perception and the Fall from Eden," in Tamar S. Gendler and John Hawthorne (eds.), *Perceptual Experience*, Oxford: Oxford University Press, 49–125.

——(2006b) "The Foundations of Two-Dimensional Semantics," in Manuel Garcia-Carpintero and Josep Macià (eds.), *Two-Dimensional Semantics: Foundations and Applications*, Oxford: Oxford University Press, 55–140.

——(2012) *Constructing the World*, Oxford: Oxford University Press.

——(2014) "Frontloading and Fregean Sense: Reply to Neta, Schroeter, and Stanley," *Analysis* 74 (4): 676–697.

Correia, Fabrice, and Benjamin Schnieder (2012) *Metaphysical Grounding: Understanding the Structure of Reality*, Cambridge: Cambridge University Press.

Dainton, Barry (2000/2006) *Stream of Consciousness: Unity and Continuity in Conscious Experience*, London: Routledge.

Dennett, Daniel C., and Marcel Kinsbourne (1992) "Time and the Observer," *Behavioral and Brain Sciences* 15 (2): 183–201.

Dretske, Fred I. (1969) *Seeing and Knowing*, Chicago: University of Chicago Press.

——(1993) "Conscious Experience," *Mind* 102 (406): 263–283.

Ellis, Willis Davis (1938) *Source Book of Gestalt Psychology*, London: Kegan Paul.

Evans, Gareth (1982) *The Varieties of Reference*, Oxford: Oxford University Press.

Farkas, Katalin (2008a) "Phenomenal Intentionality without Compromise," *Monist* 91 (2): 273–293.

——(2008b) *The Subject's Point of View*, Oxford: Oxford University Press.

Fodor, Jerry A. (1987) *Psychosemantics: The Problem of Meaning in the Philosophy of Mind*, Cambridge, MA: MIT Press.

Frege, Gottlob (1948) "Sense and Reference," *Philosophical Review* 57 (3): 209–230.

——(1956) "The Thought: A Logical Inquiry," *Mind* 65 (259): 289–311.

Gallagher, Shaun, and Dan Zahavi (2012) *The Phenomenological Mind*, London: Routledge.

Geach, Peter (1969) "What Do We Think With?" in *God and the Soul*, South Bend, IN: St. Augustine's Press, 3–41.

Goldman, Alvin (1993) "Consciousness, Folk Psychology, and Cognitive Science," *Consciousness and Cognition* 2 (4): 364–382.

Gurwitsch, Aron (1964) *The Field of Consciousness*, Pittsburgh, PA: Duquesne University Press.

——(1966) *Studies in Phenomenology and Psychology*, Evanston, IL: Northwestern University Press.

Hardy, Godfrey Harold (1992) *A Mathematician's Apology*, Cambridge: Cambridge University Press.

Harman, Gilbert (1990) "The Intrinsic Quality of Experience," *Philosophical Perspectives* 4: 31–52.

Hawley, Katherine, and Fiona Macpherson (2011) *The Admissible Contents of Experience*, Malden, MA: Wiley-Blackwell.

Horgan, Terence (2011) "From Agentive Phenomenology to Cognitive Phenomenology: A Guide for the Perplexed," in Tim Bayne and Michelle Montague (eds.), *Cognitive Phenomenology*, Oxford: Oxford University Press, 57–78.

Horgan, Terence, and George Graham (2012) "Phenomenal Intentionality and Content Determinacy," in Richard Schantz (ed.), *Prospects for Meaning*, Berlin: De Gruyter.

Horgan, Terence E., and John L. Tienson (2002) "The Intentionality of Phenomenology and the Phenomenology of Intentionality," in David J. Chalmers (ed.), *Philosophy of Mind: Classical and Contemporary Readings*, Oxford: Oxford University Press, 520–533.

Horgan, Terence E., John L. Tienson, and George Graham (2006) "Internal-World Skepticism and the Self-Presentational Nature of Phenomenal Consciousness," in Uriah Kriegel and Kenneth Williford (eds.), *Self-Representational Approaches to Consciousness*, Cambridge, MA: MIT Press, 41–61.

Husserl, Edmund (1982) *Ideas Pertaining to a Pure Phenomenology and to a Phenomenological Philosophy*, Book 1: *General Introduction to a Pure Phenomenology*, The Hague: Martinus Nijhoff.

——(1997) *Thing and Space*, vol. 7 of *Collected Works*, Dordrecht: Kluwer.

Jacobson, Daniel (2011) "Fitting Attitude Theories of Value," in Edward N. Zalta (ed.), *The Stanford Encyclopedia of Philosophy* (Spring 2011 ed.), <http://plato.stanford.edu/entries/fitting-attitude-theories/>.

Jago, Mark (2014) The Impossible: An Essay on Hyperintensionality, Oxford: Oxford University Press.

James, William (1983) *The Principles of Psychology*, Cambridge, MA: Harvard University Press.

Jenkins, C. S. I. (2011) "Is Metaphysical Dependence Irreflexive?" *Monist* 94 (2): 267-276.

Koffka, Kurt (1935) *The Principles of Gestalt Psychology*, London: Routledge & Kegan Paul.

Koksvik, Ole (2011) "Intuition," diss., Australian National University.

Kriegel, Uriah (2009) *Subjective Consciousness: A Self-Representational Theory*, Oxford: Oxford University Press.

——(2011) *The Sources of Intentionality*, Oxford: Oxford University Press.

——(2013) "The Phenomenal Intentionality Research Program," in U. Kriegel (ed.), *Phenomenal Intentionality*, Oxford: Oxford University Press, 1–26.

——(Forthcoming) *The Varieties of Consciousness*, Oxford: Oxford University Press.

Kriegel, Uriah, and Kenneth Williford (eds.) (2006) *Self-Representational Approaches to Consciousness*, Cambridge, MA: MIT Press.

Kripke, Saul A. (1980) *Naming and Necessity*, Cambridge, MA: Harvard University Press.

——(1982) *Wittgenstein on Rules and Private Language*, Cambridge, MA: Harvard University Press.

Lakatos, Imre (1976) *Proofs and Refutations: The Logic of Mathematical Discovery*, Cambridge: Cambridge University Press.

LePore, Ernest, and Barry M. Loewer (1986) "Solipsistic Semantics," *Midwest Studies in Philosophy* 10 (1): 595–614.

Levine, Joseph (2011) "On the Phenomenology of Thought," in Tim Bayne and Michelle Montague (eds.), *Cognitive Phenomenology*, Oxford: Oxford University Press, 103–120.

Loar, Brian (2003) "Phenomenal Intentionality as the Basis of Mental Content," in Martin Hahn and B. Ramberg (eds.), *Reflections and Replies: Essays on the Philosophy of Tyler Burge*, Cambridge, MA: MIT Press, 229–258.

Lormand, Eric (1996) "Nonphenomenal Consciousness," *Noûs* 30 (2): 242–261.

Lycan, William G. (1996) *Consciousness and Experience*, Cambridge, MA: MIT Press.

Mason, Elinor (2011) "Value Pluralism," in Edward N. Zalta (ed.), *The Stanford Encyclopedia of Philosophy* (Fall 2011 ed.), <http://plato.stanford.edu/entries/value-pluralism/>.

McDowell, John (1979) "Virtue and Reason," *Monist* 62 (3): 331–350.

——(1981) "Anti-Realism and the Epistemology of Understanding," in Herman Parret and Jacques Bouveresse (eds.), *Meaning and Understanding*, Berlin: De Gruyter, 225–248.

——(1984) "Wittgenstein on Following a Rule," *Synthese* 58 (March): 325–364.

——(1986) "Singular Thought and the Extent of 'Inner Space,'" in John McDowell and Philip Pettit (eds.), *Subject, Thought, and Context*, Oxford: Clarendon Press.

——(1994) *Mind and World*, Cambridge, MA: Harvard University Press.

——(1998) *Meaning, Knowledge, and Reality*, Cambridge, MA: Harvard University Press.

MacFarlane, John (2005) "The Assessment Sensitivity of Knowledge Attributions," in *Oxford Studies in Epistemology*, vol. 1, Oxford: Oxford University Press, 197–233.

McGurk, Harry, and MacDonald, John (1976) "Hearing Lips and Seeing Voices," *Nature* 264: 246–248.

Mendola, Joseph (2008) *Anti-externalism*, Oxford: Oxford University Press.

Mill, John Stuart (1987) *Utilitarianism and Other Essays*, London: Penguin Books.

Montague, Michelle (2010) "Recent Work on Intentionality," *Analysis* 70 (4): 765–782.

Neta, Ram (2014) "Chalmers' Frontloading Argument for A Priori Scrutability," *Analysis* 74 (4): 651–661.

Nida-Rümelin, Martine (2011) "Phenomenal Presence and Perceptual Awareness: A Subjectivist Account of Perceptual Openness to the World," *Philosophical Issues* 21 (1): 352–383.

O'Callaghan, Casey (2011) "Against Hearing Meanings," *Philosophical Quarterly* 61 (245): 783–807.

O'Shaughnessy, Brian (2000) *Consciousness and the World*, Oxford: Oxford University Press.

Palmer, Stephen E. (1990) "Modern Theories of Gestalt Perception," *Mind and Language* 5 (4): 289–323.

Pautz, Adam (2013) "Does Phenomenology Ground Mental Content?" in Uriah Kriegel (ed.), *Phenomenal Intentionality*, Oxford: Oxford University Press, 194–234.

Peacocke, Christopher (1983) *Sense and Content: Experience, Thought, and Their Relations*, Oxford: Oxford University Press.

Pitt, David (2004) "The Phenomenology of Cognition, or, What Is It Like to Think That P?" *Philosophy and Phenomenological Research* 69 (1): 1–36.

——(2009) "Intentional Psychologism," *Philosophical Studies* 146 (1): 117–138.

——(2011) "Introspection, Phenomenality, and the Availability of Intentional Content," in Tim Bayne and Michelle Montague (eds.), *Cognitive Phenomenology*, Oxford: Oxford University Press, 141–173.

Prinz, Jesse (2011) "The Sensory Basis of Cognitive Phenomenology," in Tim Bayne and Michelle Montague (eds.), *Cognitive Phenomenology*, Oxford: Oxford University Press, 174–196.

Putnam, Hilary (1975) "The Meaning of 'Meaning,'" in Keith Gunderson (ed.), *Language, Mind, and Knowledge*, Minnesota Studies in the Philosophy of Science, vol. 7: 131–193.

Quine, W. V. O. (1960) *Word and Object*, Cambridge, MA: MIT Press.

Raz, Joseph (1986) *The Morality of Freedom*, Oxford: Oxford University Press.

Rosen, Gideon (2010) "Metaphysical Dependence: Grounding and Reduction," in Bob Hale and Aviv Hoffmann (eds.), *Modality: Metaphysics, Logic, and Epistemology*, Oxford: Oxford University Press, 109–136.

Rosenthal, David M. (1986) "Two Concepts of Consciousness," *Philosophical Studies* 49 (May): 329–359.

Russell, Bertrand (1903) *Principles of Mathematics*, London: Routledge.

——(1905) "On Denoting," *Mind* 14 (56): 479–493.

——(1910) "Knowledge by Acquaintance and Knowledge by Description," *Proceedings of the Aristotelian Society* 11: 108–128.

——(1912) *The Problems of Philosophy*, London: Home University Library.

Schaffer, Jonathan (2009) "On What Grounds What," in David Manley, David J. Chalmers, and Ryan Wasserman (eds.), *Metametaphysics: New Essays on the Foundations of Ontology*, Oxford: Oxford University Press, 347–383.

Schroeter, L. (2014) "Scrutability and Epistemic Updating." *Analysis* 74 (4): 638–651.

Schwitzgebel, Eric (2008) "The Unreliability of Naive Introspection," *Philosophical Review* 117 (2): 245–273.

Searle, John R. (1983) *Intentionality: An Essay in the Philosophy of Mind*, Cambridge: Cambridge University Press.

——(1987) "Indeterminacy, Empiricism, and the First Person," *Journal of Philosophy* 81 (March): 123–146.

Sellars, Wilfrid (1954) "Some Reflections on Language Games," *Philosophy of Science* 21 (3): 204–228.

Sider, Theodore (2011) *Writing the Book of the World*, Oxford: Oxford University Press.

Siegel, Susanna (2006a) "How Does Phenomenology Constrain Object-Seeing?" *Australasian Journal of Philosophy* 84 (3): 429–441.

——(2006b) "Subject and Object in the Contents of Visual Experience," *Philosophical Review* 115 (3): 355–388.

——(2006c) "Which Properties Are Represented in Perception?" in Tamar S. Gendler and John Hawthorne (eds.), *Perceptual Experience*, Oxford: Oxford University Press, 481–503.

——(2010) *The Contents of Visual Experience*, Oxford: Oxford University Press.

Siewert, Charles (1998) *The Significance of Consciousness*, Princeton, NJ: Princeton University Press.

——(2011) "Phenomenal Thought," in Tim Bayne and Michelle Montague (ed.), *Cognitive Phenomenology*, Oxford: Oxford University Press, 236–267.

——(2012) "On the Phenomenology of Introspection," in Declan Smithies and Daniel Stoljar (eds.), *Introspection and Consciousness*, Oxford: Oxford University Press, 129–168.

——(2013) "Speaking Up for Consciousness," in Uriah Kriegel (ed.), *Current Controversies in Philosophy of Mind*, London: Routledge, 199–221.

Sinclair, Nathalie, David Pimm, and William Higginson (eds.) (2006) *Mathematics and the Aesthetic: New Approaches to an Ancient Affinity*, New York: Springer.

Smithies, Declan (2013a) "The Significance of Cognitive Phenomenology," *Philosophy Compass* 8 (8): 731–743.

——(2013b) "The Nature of Cognitive Phenomenology," *Philosophy Compass* 8 (8): 744–754.

Snowdon, Paul F. (1990) "The Objects of Perceptual Experience," *Proceedings of the Aristotelian Society* 64: 121–150.

Soteriou, Matthew (2007) "Content and the Stream of Consciousness," *Philosophical Perspectives* 21 (1): 543–568.

——(2009) "Mental Agency, Conscious Thinking, and Phenomenal Character," in Lucy O'Brien and Matthew Soteriou (eds.), *Mental Actions*, Oxford: Oxford University Press, 231–253.

——(2013) *The Mind's Construction: The Ontology of Mind and Mental Action*, Oxford: Oxford University Press.

Spener, Maja (2011) "Disagreement about Cognitive Phenomenology," in Tim Bayne and Michelle Montague (ed.), *Cognitive Phenomenology*, Oxford: Oxford University Press, 268–284.

Stanley, Jason (2014) "Constructing Meanings,"*Analysis* 74 (4): 662–676.

Stocker, Michael (1997) "Abstract and Concrete Value: Plurality, Conflict, and Maximization," in Ruth Chang (ed.), *Incommensurability, Incomparability and Practical Reason*, Cambridge, MA: Harvard University Press, 196–214.

Strawson, Galen (1994) *Mental Reality*, Cambridge, MA: MIT Press.

——(2011) "Cognitive Phenomenology: Real Life," in Tim Bayne and Michelle Montague (eds.), *Cognitive Phenomenology*, Oxford: Oxford University Press, 285–325.

Thomasson, Amie L. (2000) "After Brentano: A One-Level Theory of Consciousness," *European Journal of Philosophy* 8 (2): 190–210.

Thompson, Brad J. (2010) "The Spatial Content of Experience," *Philosophy and Phenomenological Research* 81 (1): 146–184.

Trogdon, Kelly (2013) "An Introduction to Grounding," in Miguel Hoeltje, Benjamin Schnieder, and Alex Steinberg (eds.), *Varieties of Dependence:*

Ontological Dependence, Grounding, Supervenience, Response-Dependence, Basic Philosophical Concepts, Munich: Philosophia, 97–122.

Tye, Michael (1995) *Ten Problems of Consciousness: A Representational Theory of the Phenomenal Mind*, Cambridge, MA: MIT Press.

——(2003) *Consciousness and Persons: Unity and Identity*, Cambridge, MA: MIT Press.

——(2009) *Consciousness Revisited: Materialism Without Phenomenal Concepts*, Cambridge, MA: MIT Press.

Tye, Michael, and Briggs Wright (2011) "Is There a Phenomenology of Thought?" in Tim Bayne and Michelle Montague (eds.), *Cognitive Phenomenology*, Oxford: Oxford University Press, 326–344.

Watzl, Sebastian (2011) "Attention as Structuring of the Stream of Consciousness," in Christopher Mole, Declan Smithies, and Wayne Wu (eds.), *Attention: Philosophical and Psychological Essays*, Oxford: Oxford University Press, 145–173.

Williamson, Timothy (2007) *The Philosophy of Philosophy*, Malden, MA: Blackwell.

Yablo, Stephen (1993) "Is Conceivability a Guide to Possibility?" *Philosophy and Phenomenological Research* 53 (1): 1–42.

Zahavi, Dan (2005) *Subjectivity and Selfhood: Investigating the First-Person Perspective*, Cambridge, MA: MIT Press.

INDEX